The
Power of
Business
EN ESPAÑOL

The
Power of
Business

EN ESPAÑOL

7 Fundamental Keys to Unlocking the Potential
of the Spanish-Language Hispanic Market

José Cancela

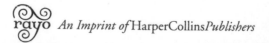

An Imprint of HarperCollins*Publishers*

HarperCollins books may be purchased for educational, business, or sales promotional use. For information, please write: Special Markets Department, HarperCollins Publishers, 10 East 53rd Street, New York, NY 10022.

FIRST EDITION

Designed by Daniel Lagin

Library of Congress Cataloging-in-Publication Data has been applied for.
ISBN: 978-0-06-123499-6

07   08   09   10   11   ID/RRD   10   9   8   7   6   5   4   3   2

Dedicated to my daughter Yvanna and my son Carlos . . .
road trips forever . . . Sierra Mist Yaaa . . .
Marcelo and Isabella, Splash Mountain, here we come . . .
again . . .

Contents

Introduction

Imagine discovering a treasure chest stuffed with nearly $1 trillion, right in your backyard. But you can't just break it open. If you try smashing your way in, you don't get the cash. You need a key.

That's what this book is all about. The U.S. Hispanic market is closing in on $1 trillion in buying power. In sheer numbers, it's already twice the size of Australia. And growing. Right here in your backyard.

There are nearly 43 million Latinos in the United States, according to the latest U.S. Census estimates. And the number is increasing faster than any other segment. Hispanics accounted for nearly half of all the growth in the nation between 2004 and 2005. Census projections predict that between now and 2050 we'll add about 2.5 Hispanics to the population every minute. Every minute! That's nearly 3,700 a day. That's the equivalent of adding a Berkeley, Calif., a Killeen, Tex, or an Ann

Arbor, Mich., worth of Latinos every month. Or, if you take it a step further, like adding a Phoenix or a Philadelphia full of Hispanics every year, from now until mid-century.

You get it. The Hispanic market is big. And getting bigger, fast.

But knowing that isn't enough. Here's a contrarian, and vital, fact: Even though more than half of them will be born in this country, outnumbering the number of immigrants coming in from other places, more than two-thirds will speak Spanish. Study after study shows that, unlike previous waves of immigrant groups in this country, third-generation Latinos continue to cling to their language and culture.

What's more, Spanish isn't just the language we speak, it's the language that speaks to us. It connects with us in ways English just can't, on an emotional level, even if we are what is known as "English-dominant,"—meaning we speak and communicate primarily and predominantly in that language. We identify with Spanish, even as it identifies us.

Starting to sound scary? Too complicated? It doesn't have to be.

Speak to Me

Somewhere along the line, someone made this a lot harder than it has to be.

When people started talking about selling to Hispanics, they started focusing on the differences. Suddenly, it seemed that you had to speak all different kinds of Spanish. Or was it English? You had to be careful about where people were from, where they lived now; whether they were assimilated or acculturated. The list went on and on.

Well, yeah, but . . .

Birds and Bees

If we followed similar advice about dating, we'd be extinct. We'd think we had to learn molecular biology, anatomy, chemistry, and advanced psychology before we could even talk to someone of the opposite sex. If you wanted to go beyond that, it would be next to impossible.

Luckily, we know better.

The same is true of marketing and selling to Latinos: It doesn't hurt to become an expert. But you don't have to be one to succeed. You don't have to know how to build a car to drive one. You do need to know the rules of the road.

That's what we'll show you here: how to get where you want to be, without burying you in unnecessary intricacies.

Hispanics *are* different. It takes different techniques to communicate with us, to connect with us, and to sell to us. But you don't need a Ph.D. to do it.

The Power of Business en Español

The Power of Business en Español demystifies Latinos. It gives you seven simple keys to understanding the people, the culture, and the market of Spanish-language Hispanic America.

The keys are designed to be independent from one another: Each one, by itself, is potent. In combination, though, you'll find that they fit together even more powerfully. Together, they'll show you how to think about the market and how to make plans to tap into it. They'll give you what you need to expand into the Hispanic marketplace easily, with confidence, and with the power to succeed. Immediately.

The Power of Business en Español shows you how to cut through the confusing mass of data and complicated cultural gobbledygook. It teaches you how to succeed in Spanish, in plain English.

On top of that, it gives you everything you need to know to understand the forces shaping this rapidly changing sector, without burying you in unnecessary detail.

And, in it, we'll identify the growth areas of today *and* tomorrow, and show you how to target them.

In short, *The Power of Business en Español* not only tells you what's happening, but how to use it to your advantage.

It doesn't matter if you're self-employed, own your own business, or run a Fortune 500 company. *The Power of Business en Español* will work for salespeople, travel agents, real estate brokers—anyone who's selling or wants to sell their product or service to the fastest growing market sector in the country.

This book is for managers and executives who want to understand and profit from the changes in both the marketplace and the workplace, for city councilmen and U.S. senators witnessing the dramatic impact of Latinos upon their constituencies, for educators and academics seeing the changes in the classroom. Or for anyone who simply wants to learn a bit more about their new neighbors.

Short and Sweet

The Power of Business en Español is written in short, easily digestible sections.

Each chapter reveals a different aspect of Latino culture, and gives you a key to understanding and unlocking the potential of this huge and explosively dynamic market.

This isn't theory. We use real-life examples showing how different companies have succeeded or failed. We'll show you how they have recognized and used one or all of the seven keys to increase their profits, expand their brand, and beat their competition.

They have discovered that the things we have in common are much more important than the things that are different.

Successful politicians are doing the same, recognizing how

our values and the things that motivate us are the same solid American values this country is built on.

And both—the politicians who have won our votes and the companies that have earned our patronage—are learning that we are fiercely loyal.

One Step at a Time

When things seem complicated, people shy away from getting in on them at all. That's why it's important to keep it simple.

The market is there. If you miss the ride, you'll be left by the side. And if that's where you are, you're going to be left behind.

That may be why you're reading this in the first place. You've probably already noticed. The world has changed. The cheese has moved. There's a new market out there. And there's no reason to be afraid of it, or intimidated by it. Just the opposite. It's full of vitality, opportunity, and potential—and it's not going away.

If your competitor has already moved into this space, you're already behind in the game. You need to catch up. If your competitor hasn't made the move, you can gain a critical advantage by being first.

About Me

How do I know? Because I'm Hispanic. I grew up in the culture, speaking the language, right here in the United States.

It's not only in my blood, it's in my experience. I was very fortunate to have started as a sales trainee in 1979 at what was then called SIN, Spanish International Network, better known today as Univision. Little did I know then, that I would spend the next twenty years working with some key individuals helping define Spanish-language television broadcasting in America at both Univision and Telemundo. I was also part of a great team of broadcasters that created the first Spanish-language talk radio network in America. I also lived out a lifelong dream of holding public office by running for mayor of Miami-Dade County, Florida. I was not victorious but it taught me a great deal.

Most recently, I took those decades of experience and formed a full-service Hispanic market consulting firm, Hispanic USA Inc., with offices in Miami and San Antonio. *Our mission is to make it easy and profitable for our clients to understand and market to Hispanics in the United States.*

In the twenty-five years I've been doing this, I've worked with Latinos all across the United States—in the Heartland, the South, and both coasts.

I've been in the front lines as the market has evolved. I've helped companies and individuals succeed in it, and worked side by side watching and learning from the success of others. I've also seen plenty fail, and understood the reasons why.

That's what led to this book. I teamed up with Carlos Harrison because of his knowledge of the print side. He's the former deputy managing editor of *People en Español*, the number one Spanish-language magazine in the country.

By the Numbers

This book is not heavy on numbers. It gives you useful information, information that helps you see how big things are, and where they are. It's all you need to know.

What's important here are the concepts and the trends. And that's what I focus on. They are keys to open locks, to open doors. To give you access to a market that's bigger than all of Canada, in terms of the number of people, and growing faster than any other.

Swimming with Alligators

Many have turned this market opportunity into a monster, and remain paralyzed by fear. They ignore it, avoid it, act like it doesn't matter. All because they won't adapt to the changing marketplace, or can't.

It's their loss. It shouldn't be yours.

We all know how important it is for businesses to adjust to the evolving environment. The landscape is littered with examples of those that didn't. Think of the shift to the suburbs that created a market for shopping centers and all but killed most downtowns across the country. Others see the opportunity and seize it. Think of the impact of the baby boom as it has moved through the ages, creating a youth-oriented boon for everything from rock and roll in the '60s and '70s to an increasing demand for arthritis remedies, wrinkle removers, and Viagra today.

Peter Drucker noted that "the extreme youth culture of the last forty years was based on demographics. It's an old rule that the population group that is both the biggest and growing the fastest determines the mood."

That old rule now holds true for the boomers *and* Hispanics. The boomers are the biggest, but Latinos are growing the fastest. That's an opportunity, not something to be afraid of.

Here's a different way of looking at it:

A man invites several people to his house for a party. After they're there, he takes them out back and shows them the pool. It's filled with alligators.

"Anyone who swims to the other side," he says, "can have any wish he wants."

Well, there's plenty of shuffling, mumbling, and clearing of throats—but no takers.

And they're all a bit nervous as they go back inside.

Then they hear a splash.

Everyone rushes back outside. They find a guy climbing out of the pool on the other side.

The host is as surprised as anyone, but he asks what the man wants for his wish.

"I just want to know who pushed me," the man says.

The moral: Some get pushed by the competition. Some take the plunge by themselves. However it happens, everyone who dives in finds that it's not as bad—or as difficult—as they imagined. They've done it. So can you.

Diving In

The information in *The Power of Business en Español* will show you how to tap into the Spanish-language market—and succeed—right now. It will show you where the opportunities are, how to tailor your offerings to the marketplace, and how to attract and keep customers. Right now.

It will also show you how you can go deeper, drill down, and add layers to your marketing plan or make it more refined to target specific segments.

In *The Power of Business en Español* you will learn that you don't have to stay out of the market just because you're not an expert in every nuance, every tiny cultural difference, or every subtlety of the Spanish language.

In Chapter One, "We All Use the Same Dictionary," I'll give you the first key. I'll show you that Spanish is a lot like

English—and you don't see car companies making separate commercials for Boston and Birmingham, do you? One English works just fine from Washington, D.C., to Washington State. It's no different in Spanish.

Equally important, I'll also show you how to stay out of trouble. That's what can happen when people try to make things more complicated than they have to be. I'll show you some examples.

With the next key, "We're Everywhere," I'll show you how the demographic shift is happening all across the country—in small towns and large cities, from the coasts to the Heartland. The explosion is so staggering that it's turning some places into hyper-growth markets. They include the area known as the Triangle, around Raleigh, Durham, and Chapel Hill. But even such unlikely places as Minneapolis, Omaha, Des Moines, and Portland saw their Latino populations double, triple, and more.

I'll also show you how to spot the signs of the Latino influence in your neighborhood so that you can position yourself to take advantage of it.

The third chapter, "We Love the U.S.A." is the third key. I'll show you that Latinos believe in the American Dream, and they come here for the same reason the Founding Fathers did, to build a better life. What does that mean to you? We want the same things you do, and we're willing to work for them.

Home ownership among Hispanics is growing faster than for any other group in the country—twice as fast as non-Hispanic whites and four times as fast as African-Americans.

Of course, that's good news for banks offering mortgages, furniture companies, and a whole host of other businesses connected to housing, directly or indirectly. Everybody from Ikea to the corner lamp shop, Home Depot to the neighborhood hardware store, Sears and the local appliance store makes money off homebuyers, sooner or later. So do plumbers, electricians, and the other repairmen who get called for help.

Entrepreneurial Latinos are starting businesses at a phenomenal rate as well—three times the national average. There are about two million Hispanic-owned businesses in the country. And that's expected to double every five years. In 2004, those businesses generated close to $300 billion in sales. Anyone in business-to-business knows those entrepreneurs need everything from vehicles to computers to office supplies, and a slew of other products and services.

The next key, "We Vote," is about a lot more than politics. It's important for politicians, of course, to recognize that with more than 10 million registered voters, Latinos control a critical sway vote. George W. Bush knew Hispanics could make the difference, and he deliberately targeted them. But every businessperson can benefit from recognizing that Latinos believe in a very personal relationship with their elected officials. I'll show you how you can use that knowledge to turn your elected official into your assistant marketing manager, promoting your product or service to influential decision makers in the Latino community, and opening doors for new business.

After that comes "We Have Strong Family Values." Knowing this can help you make your advertising more effective. Family comes first, and the center of the family is Mom. She's the decision maker. Target her if you want to reach anyone in the family. With this key, you'll also see how major retailers and grocery store chains capitalize on the fact that Latinos stick together, and shop together.

It may sound funny, but it really is true: "We Want to Be Courted in the Language We Make Love In." It's a vital key for connecting with Hispanics. As I said before, Spanish speaks to us in a special way, even when we speak English most of the time. It's our number one hot button, whether we're born here or someplace else. Like most consumers, our emotions shape our decisions. Spanish connects with us on an emotional level. It builds trust. It builds affection. Even when you don't speak it very well, we tend to like you for trying.

And that doesn't change significantly with Latinos who grow up here and speak English as fluently as you do. Studies repeatedly have shown that even third-generation Hispanics, whose parents were born here as well, buck the trends of previous immigrant groups. Rather than shedding the language of their parents and grandparents, they revel in it. According to a McKinsey & Co. study, more than 67 percent of the Latino population of the United States will consist of bilingual Hispanics in 2010.

The point is this: If you think you can reach us effectively in English only, you're wrong. In Chapter Six, we'll show you how to do it right.

The last key is "We Have Real Buying Power." That's the one about the $1 trillion treasure chest and how you can dig in with both hands if you know what you're doing. I use case studies and real-life examples to show you how some corporate giants (and some not so giant ones) have succeeded. And how some got it wrong.

We do spend a lot on cleansers, and toothpaste, and disposable diapers. Latinos spend significantly more on gas, motor oil, men's and children's clothing, footwear, housewares, sports, and toys. In this chapter, I'll detail how Hispanics over-index in their spending on a variety of things, and how knowing that can help you. I'll also identify business sectors with significant growth potential, thanks to Latino spending patterns.

In short, *The Power of Business en Español* will show you how to dive into the market and thrive right now. You won't get eaten by alligators. And you don't have to swim the English Channel. If you want to later on, great. But I'll show you how you can do well right now.

The
Power of
Business
EN ESPAÑOL

Chapter 1

WE ALL USE THE SAME DICTIONARY

They don't make a different *Friends* for Boston and Alabama, another for Texas and yet another for Seattle. They don't have to. The viewers in Atlanta may speak with a different drawl than the viewers in Brooklyn, but they all understand the same English.

The same is true in Spanish. We all use the same dictionary.

English-language television tends to use a very vanilla, middle-of-the-road, could-be-from-anywhere way of talking. Take a look at some talk shows, for example. Ever listen carefully to the late Johnny Carson? He was from Iowa. Dave Letterman is from Indiana. Jay Leno is from New York. They each have their own style. But their accents are practically indistinguishable. You don't hear Leno saying, "Fuggedaboutit!" Unless it's part of a joke.

Look at the network news. They didn't substitute Tom Brokaw with someone from Kentucky for a reason. Not that we have anything against people from Kentucky, but that sweet bluegrass drawl just doesn't play well across the country. Peter Jennings was from Canada, but it was impossible to tell from his accent.

The English-language networks want to use a language everyone is comfortable with. They know you need to create a comfort level because you want the most acceptance from the most people.

And it's not just the accent. You don't hear a lot of regional slang on English-language TV. Jeff Foxworthy might say, "That dog don't hunt," but you won't hear it from a lot of other people. Everybody on TV pretty much uses the same English. And everybody watching at home understands.

Spanish works the same way.

The networks use a fairly standard Spanish whether a show is produced in Mexico, Venezuela, L.A., or Miami. And everyone understands.

Oh, we might hear the lilt that differentiates a Mexican accent from a Cuban one, or note the way a Puerto Rican pronounces her R's. And, because so many shows are set in Mexico and the directors want to give them a realistic sense of place, they might use typically Mexican expressions in them. But generally, the networks know their shows have to play to a diverse cross section (and, with most of the shows, in many different Spanish-speaking countries), so they stick with middle-of-the-road Spanish.

The newscasts use it. Smart advertisers use it.

Walter Cronkite Spanish

More often than not, when people start talking about what it takes to create a marketing campaign targeting U.S. Latinos, one of the first things they say is, "Well, you know, when you're dealing with the West Coast and the East Coast, you have to use different dialects."

They're wrong. The commonly held belief that we have to speak different forms of Spanish to communicate with Hispanics in different parts of the U.S.A. is just not true. It's a myth—it's people making things harder than they have to be.

Worrying about accents becomes a barrier for folks. How will they pick the right one for the right place? How many different ones will they have to worry about?

They start seeing all kinds of financial implications. All of a sudden, they see themselves having to produce not one TV spot, but two, three . . . dozens. And then, "Oh my God! How much money will that cost? Oh, no, no, no." And they start multiplying in their heads, and . . .

The next thing you know, they're already convincing themselves that marketing in Spanish is not a good idea because this is just going to be too expensive. If they can't reach Latinos in English, they just won't bother. Forget how massive the Spanish-speaking Hispanic market is. Forget how underserved and untapped it is. Forget how lucrative it is. All they can think is, "It can't be worth it. It's just too difficult. I don't know what return on the investment I'm going to have."

The good news is, the folks who think that they have to use "dialects" won't be your competition. They build their own barrier. While they stay where they are, you get to dive in. And, as you pass them on your way to the bank, you'll hear them saying, "It can't be worth it. It's just too difficult."

There *are* different accents, not dialects, but you don't have to use them. They're a minefield. And there's no reason to force yourself to tiptoe through a minefield when you don't have to. Going around it is better. It's easier, faster, and there's a much smaller risk of things blowing up in your face.

The truth is, we all work out of the same dictionary. We share a common language understood by Latinos in Dallas, L.A., New York, and Miami. We call it: "Walter Cronkite Spanish." It's a neutral Spanish that doesn't use regional slang terms or uncommon idiomatic expressions. In "Walter Cronkite Spanish" a bus is an *autobús*, not a *gua-gua*, as a Cuban might call it.

Turn on Your Radio

Radio is no different, in any language.

For years, one of the most popular Spanish-language morning radio programs in L.A.—where 63.5 percent of the Latinos are of Mexican descent—has been hosted by *El Cucuy de la Ma-ñana*, Renán Almendárez Coello. Yet chances are that a good chunk of his faithful listeners don't know he's from Honduras. And if they do, they don't care. It doesn't matter. His listeners don't have to learn "Honduran." He talks. They get it.

So, if these mega-money-making machines—the television and radio networks—use the same Spanish to communicate with their millions upon millions of viewers and listeners, why would you do it any differently?

There are some pretty smart people running those businesses. They've spent a lot of time thinking about how to attract and reach an audience. The best way, they've decided, is by sticking with a common Spanish, a "Walter Cronkite Spanish." They know it works. Their ratings prove it day after day and night after night.

They know that we come from different places. They know that, with a practiced ear, you might be able to tell that someone comes from Colombia instead of Venezuela, or from Mexico instead of Argentina. Even a less-practiced listener might notice that the first three pronounce the *ll* sound (as in the word *calle*, or street) like a y, while the Argentine's sounds more like a *j*.

But they know it doesn't matter that much when it comes to delivering a message. People from those places all understand each other perfectly, especially as they have become part of Hispanic U.S.A.

<u>You Say Tomato</u>

It's not just the language of the networks. There's a common "networking language" that connects Latinos and Hispanics, whether they're in San Francisco, Miami, or Memphis.

When we get together, we tend to drop the Spanish versions of "Fuggedaboutit!"

Venezuelans may use the word "*chamo*" for a male friend. Mexicans might say "*cuate*." But when a Mexican, a Venezuelan, and a Puerto Rican get together in the U.S., they're three *amigos*, and that's the word they tend to use.

And, even if one is calling his car an "*automóvil*," another, "*carro*," and a third, "*coche*," that's not going to keep them from understanding each other. It's no different than three English speakers using the terms "automobile," "car," and "vehicle." Spanish in the United States incorporates words and expressions from the many different forms of Spanish spoken here. It's perfectly fine to use *anteojos*, *gafas*, or *espejuelos* when we're talking about *lentes* (eyeglasses).

Some slang expressions may slip into the conversation here or there. Some might even be used deliberately, for effect, the same way Leno or Foxworthy tosses in a particularly distinctive "Hey, *paisan*" or "y'all." A Spanish-speaker might use the Mexican exclamation "*¡Órale!*" or the Argentine "*¡Ché!*" to make a point or to get a laugh.

For the most part, though, the group will seek common

ground with the common networking language. The same holds true in business dealings. Maybe even more so.

When Hispanics from different places come together for negotiations, they don't have to call for an interpreter. But they do tend to drop their idiomatic expressions. The talk doesn't have to be formal, but it has to be clear. And the best way to make sure everybody knows what everybody is talking about is to speak in Spanish everyone understands.

Tongue Twisters

Oh, sure, there are regional variations. And they're important to keep in mind.

They can even be useful, in certain applications. But be careful. They can be very dangerous, too.

On the useful side: You might want to employ them as part of a narrower, targeted, or grassroots-level second or third step in a marketing campaign.

A local merchant who wants to differentiate himself from a national chain by playing up the "I'm your neighbor" angle might want to use the local lingo. He might want to sprinkle his ad copy with some local expressions, pepper his pitch with words or phrases that have special significance to the audience he wants to reach.

They might even be used for effect on a broader scale. A long distance company promoting its international calling plans might deliberately have the actors in its commercials use some regional accents or words to subtly convey the idea that the calls are crossing borders to connect with "back home."

But trying to use those local idioms or regional dialects can cause more trouble than it prevents. Just ask the folks at Hershey's.

When the popular chocolate company launched a new line of flavors aimed at Latinos in the spring of 2005, it wound up putting its advertising foot in its corporate mouth.

Instead of using the generally recognizable term for sweet, condensed milk that Häagen-Dazs did just a few months earlier—*dulce de leche*—the Hershey's ads used a particularly Mexican word.

Unfortunately, most non-Mexicans don't recognize the word *cajeta*. Worse, for many of the ones who do, the word is a lewd reference to a woman's, well, womanhood.

Lost in Translation

Let's be honest. There are potential pitfalls in using general Spanish, as well.

It's comical to wonder if the "Got Milk?" people really meant to ask, "Are you lactating?" And, in stories that have grown to the status of urban legends, it did. In the official account of those involved, however, Los Angeles advertising expert Anita Santiago stepped in to save the milk folks from themselves, before they blundered.

When the California Milk Processor Board went to her for help adapting the immensely successful English-language campaign to target Latinos, Santiago pointed out that a literal translation of the slogan would be *"¿Tienes leche?"* But in Spanish, that's a rather personal question. It's the way you would ask a woman if she's producing milk for nursing. Not exactly the kind of question you want blaring in three-foot tall letters on a billboard by the side of the highway.

Santiago also pointed out an important cultural difference. Hispanics aren't as likely to drink a lot of milk by the glass. But, as we'll discuss in the chapter about family values, Latinos tend to care intensely about their children's well-being.

The solution took both the language and the cultural differences into account. Santiago helped the milk folks adapt their theme by completely changing the slogan. She focused on the underlying message they wanted to deliver, that drinking milk is good for you. And what Latino parent doesn't want her kids to be healthy? The end result: *"Familia, amor y leche"* (family, love, and milk).

A similar story involves the now defunct Braniff Airways, which wanted to promote its new leather seats on its flights to Mexico. It wanted to use the slogan, "Fly in Leather." Perfectly fine in English. As the story goes, though, the ad writers translated it into Spanish as *"Vuela Braniff. Vuela en-*

cuero." That means "Fly Braniff. Fly Naked." A novel suggestion—and an interesting way of attracting passengers—but hardly what the airline had in mind.

What happened was that they left out the space between *en*, which means "in," and *cuero*, which means "leather." Joined together, you get a whole new word, *encuero*, which means "naked."

Sometimes the problem comes from using words that have worked their way into English, so we think we know what they mean in Spanish.

That's how Volkswagen caused a furor just this past year with an ad campaign announcing that its GTI 2006 model had "Turbo-Cojones."

Cojones has migrated into use in English as slang for gutsy or daring. And that was what the advertising agency was aiming for when it ordered up bold, black-and-white billboards with the slogan in big letters. But in Spanish *cojones* means "testicles." Displayed in giant letters looming over Miami's densely Hispanic neighborhood of Little Havana, the words proclaiming the car had "Turbo-Testicles" provoked an immediate outcry. The ad had to be pulled within days.

The Name Game

Even your product or brand name can cause *cajeta*-style problems as it makes its way from one language to another.

When Mitsubishi introduced the car most of us in the United States know as the Montero, it was known as the Pajero. It still is in Japan and most of Europe. You'll see it entered, and often winning, under that name in the grueling off-road Dakar Rally. But sturdy and capable as the vehicle is, Mitsubishi quickly learned that the name wasn't going to help its sales in Latin America or to U.S. Hispanics. It might even hurt. Because to a significant portion of Spanish speakers, the word *pajero* means "a man who masturbates." One version of the car model bore the designation Pajero iO. The name, a company press release stated, was meant to convey the sense of the Italian word *io*, which means I or me. In short, "I, masturbator."

The carmaker correctly realized that television commercial images of a rugged man or a smiling father and suburban family spilling out of the car take on a whole new connotation when paired with the label "Pajero."

Mitsubishi did the smart thing. In Spain and the Americas, it released the car under the name we recognize in the United States. The new name, Montero, means "mountain man," conveying an image of handsome ruggedness better suited to the four-wheel drive sport-utility vehicle.

Speaking in Tongues

The point is this: Bad translations are bad business.

Don't trust your translation to just anyone. And don't trust it to a computer program. Hire a professional. You wouldn't let the maintenance staff write your ad copy in English, would you? Why would you trust your translation to your electrician just because he speaks Spanish?

And don't rely on a software program to do it. You've seen those instructions that come with things made overseas that read: "Slot B to insert A in." Computer translations tend to turn out that way. The words are right, but the grammar ends up sounding like Yoda in *Star Wars*.

You want a professional translator. Here are some things to keep in mind when you're picking one:

First off, you want a native Spanish speaker. It's always better when someone translates into his mother tongue. You know this from your own personal experience. You've heard a non-native English speaker translate something from their native language. No matter how long they've been speaking English, or how well they do it, the translation can come out a little stilted or awkward. It's correct, no doubt. But the word choices might seem a little off, not quite the way someone who grew up speaking English would say it.

Or they might not know certain American idiomatic expressions. In English, something expensive costs "an arm and a leg." In Spanish it's "*un ojo de la cara*." Literally, that's "an eye from the face." The sentiment is there, but tangled, and a bit shocking. A straight translation of "egg on your face" would be even worse. You could quickly end up in a Turbo-Cojones situation, since the straight translation for eggs is Spanish slang for testicles.

It's good if the translator has an education in translation, but it's even more important that they have lots of experience.

Also, look for someone who specializes in the type of translation you want. Medical terminology requires one way of thinking, marketing calls for another. Ad copy uses word play and symbolism that stirs up layers of thought and appeals to emotions. A real "feel" for what you want to say is crucial for the translation to turn out right.

Make sure your translator knows "Walter Cronkite Spanish." Unless you're going for effect, as I mentioned before, you'll want to stick with the neutral, networking Spanish.

Have at least one native Spanish speaker from a different country proofread the translation. Preferably more. The greater the variety of Spanish dialects that come into play to read over your translation, the more likely you are to avoid pitfalls like *cajeta*.

Simple Pleasures

Those kinds of slipups are easy to avoid. The more critical issue is the central theme of this book: Don't make it harder than it has to be.

You don't need to build a rocket ship to get to the corner market; your own two feet will do. The rocket may work, but you're making getting to the store much more difficult and problematic than it needs to be. It will take more time, cost more money, and have a much greater chance of failing.

The rocket may be a beautiful thing to behold when it's done—sleek and powerful. But you've got to wonder: Was it worth the work? By the time you finish putting on that last coat of paint and firing the engines, your neighbors—and your competition—have been to the store and back a thousand times or more.

The same is true of Spanish. It doesn't have to be complicated. The keys to a successful slogan are the same in any language. You want it to reach your market. You want it to motivate people to do something: to buy, take action—something. It helps if it's memorable. Those principles apply in English or Spanish. The target market changes. The language changes. The principles don't.

Repeat after us: The rules remain the same. The rules remain the same. The rules . . .

That doesn't mean everything that works in English will

work in Spanish. Some things may. Some may not. Some may work a little. Some may even work better. But that's a reflection of the message, not the language.

"Family, Love, and Milk" may work better than "Got Milk?" for a variety of reasons. But both have the same aim, and both have the same thinking behind them. They want to connect with the people in the target audience, and get them to buy milk.

Both succeed well in their respective languages. And both work equally well with everyone in their respective target markets. The English version of the slogan didn't have to be adapted for the people in Chicago. They didn't reword it for folks in Georgia. The same Spanish version played in El Paso and in Brooklyn. And it worked in both places.

The fact is, they may play more country and western music on the radio in Nashville, and more hip hop in New York, but the Cadillac commercials you see are the same in both places.

In the same way, you may find more *norteño* playing in San Diego and more *merengue* in New York, but the bottom line is: It's the Spanish that's music to our ears.

In Plain Spanish

What's important is that you deliver your message in the language we're listening in. That's Spanish.

When you do, remember the key: We all use the same dictionary.

You don't have to get hung up on the nuances. Don't worry about regional subtleties. Regionalisms can blow up in your face.

A "universal Spanish" reaches the broadest universe. So use a professional translator who knows "Walter Cronkite Spanish," who gets the "feel" of what you're trying to say and who understands that the best translations keep culture, context, and intention foremost. And get at least one other native Spanish speaker to proofread your copy.

Chapter 2

WE'RE EVERYWHERE

Forget the Baby Boom. The *Bebé* Boom is here.

At 42.7 million and counting, there are more Hispanics in the United States than there are Canadians in Canada. That's twice the population of Australia. And that doesn't include the 4 million living in Puerto Rico.

Put them all together, and that's more than the population of California. More than all of Texas and New York combined.

In all, U.S. Latinos make up the second largest Hispanic nation in the world. Bigger than Spain. Bigger than Colombia. Second only to Mexico.

That's a huge market, right in our own backyard.

And it's growing. No, not growing, exploding.

Hispanics are the fastest growing market in the United States. Mostly young, the Latino population in the U.S. is increasing at a rate four times faster than the national average.

In part, it's because of immigration. In part, it's procreation.

Bebé Boom

Hispanics are young compared to the general population. A full 34 percent are 18 or younger, compared with one-fourth for non-Hispanics. Overall, the median age of Hispanics is 27.2, compared to 36.2 for the general population.

These young Latinos are, in most cases, just coming into their highest earning years. They're shopping for homes, building brand loyalties—and creating the next wave of U.S. Hispanics. Right now, one of every five babies born in the United States is Hispanic, one of every two in California. That helps explain why we over-index on spending on disposable diapers. But it's also a clear indicator of the future.

Latinos have birth rates twice as high as those of non-Hispanics. In the years ahead, that fertility will continue to outweigh immigration as the primary cause of Hispanic population growth. The number of Hispanic children has almost doubled since 1980, and today half of the children of Latino immigrants are 11 or younger. It's no surprise that Hispanics buy significantly more toys than non-Hispanics.

And, since a greater number of Latinos are in their childbearing years than non-Hispanics, the impact is only going to grow greater.

Hispanics accounted for nearly half the nation's population growth between 2000 and 2005. In just the year between July 1, 2004, and July 1, 2005, the nation grew by 2.8 million people. Hispanics counted for 1.3 million, or 49 percent, of them.

More importantly, the census bureau reported that 800,000 of those "was because of natural increase (births minus deaths) and 500,000 was because of immigration."

The tide shifted in the 1990s. Before that, immigrants accounted for most of the Latino population increase every year. But in the 1990s, the number of Hispanics born here overtook foreign-born immigrants as the leading source of Hispanic population growth.

That's creating what some experts have termed a "tamale in the snake," or a demographic bulge of youthful Hispanics.

Latinos will account for two-thirds of the nation's high school population growth over the next decade. By 2020, the Hispanic teen population is expected to grow 62 percent, compared to a mere 10 percent growth for teens overall.

Soon, those kids will start having kids of their own. So no matter what happens with U.S. immigration policy, the number of Latinos will continue to grow dramatically.

As a result, Roberto Suro of the Pew Hispanic Center and Jeffrey S. Passel of the Urban Institute concluded:

"Between 2000 and 2020, the number of second-generation Latinos in U.S. schools will double and the number in the U.S. labor force will triple. Nearly one-fourth of labor force growth over the next twenty years will be from children of Latino immigrants."

They projected that the second-generation would increase from 9.8 million in 2000 to 21.7 million in 2020. The number of second-generation children between five- and nineteen-years old, at 11 million in 2005, is expected to hit 16 million by 2020.

It makes what *Latina* magazine founder Christy Haubegger told *Newsweek* ring all the more true: "The [African-American] civil-rights slogan was 'We shall overcome.' Ours is going to be 'We shall overwhelm.'"

COMING TO A THEATER NEAR YOU

It's not just happening in the places you'd expect, like Texas or Miami. It's happening in Atlanta, and Tacoma, and Little Rock, Ark.

Hispanics have accounted for 78 percent of the growth in the top 15 metro markets in the U.S. since 1980. Phenomenal as that is, it pales in comparison to the rates of growth in other parts of the country. Overall, Latinos are expected to supply nearly half of the country's total growth over the next fifteen years, and hit 60 million by 2020.

In the first fifty years of this century alone, the U.S. Census Bureau predicts that the number of Hispanics in the nation will nearly triple. According to its projections, another 67 million Latinos will be added to the nearly 43 million already here.

So what?

With numbers, come dollars. Latino buying power is growing twice as fast as the rest of the population's. It's expected to
hit $1 trillion by 2010, up from $686 billion today.

There's more. According to the Pew Research Center, "The
impact of Latino population growth is magnified by the fact
that the white and African-American populations are not only
stable in size but also aging. As the huge baby boom generation
moves toward retirement, young Latinos are filling in behind
them."

That means opportunity for those willing to seize it.

In the spring of 2006, a group of bankers, marketers, and
government officials gathered for a full-day conference about
the explosive growth of the Latino market. They discussed how
to tap into the massive financial potential of this "unbanked"
demographic.

The place: Minnesota. That's right, Minnesota.

"The First Annual Emerging Markets Conference," hosted
by the Minnesota Bankers Association, included sessions on
"Spanish for Bankers," "Cultural Competency," and "Marketing to U.S. Latinos." The attendees heard about the Emerging
Markets Home ownership Initiative, a collaborative public-
private program aimed at increasing the number of minority
homeowners in Minnesota "significantly and dramatically" by
2010.

Small wonder they're paying so much attention. In that
state alone, Hispanics now have $1.9 billion worth of consumer

buying power. The Latino population there nearly tripled between 1990 and 2002, from 54,000 to 158,700. And while
most live in the seven-county cluster of the Twin Cities Metro
Area, Latinos now live in every one of the state's eighty-seven
counties.

Minnesota may be one of the last places people would
name when they're thinking of Hispanics. But what's happening there is an example of what's happening all across the
country. Markets are changing fast, and smart businesses are
moving to meet the challenge—or slipping to the sidelines
while their competitors do.

From Little Rock to Las Vegas, Wichita to West Palm Beach,
surging Latino populations are forming lucrative new markets
or, sometimes, changing the character of existing markets so
dramatically that businesses risk extinction if they don't adapt.

DRIVING CHANGE

In an interview with *Business Week* Online, former HUD Secretary Henry Cisneros pointed out the impact of the demographic shift:

"The auto industry is looking at a dramatic leveling of sales
as the boomers reach their mid-fifties and slow down their car
buying. If you take the Latinos out, you see flat to no growth.
Add the Latinos, and the car market grows 100,000 vehicles per
year. You're seeing companies making decisions based on that."

Toyota, he said, responded by building an auto-making

plant in San Antonio. The goal: to be closer to Latinos, and to have them as part of their workforce.

"Every company," Cisneros said, "wants to appeal to a demographic that is younger and with families that are larger."

Many companies will have to change their whole way of thinking. They'll have to realize it's not just about allocating dollars for Hispanic marketing efforts in five markets. It's about beefing up all across the country. Maybe, in some areas, even in advance of this growth, no matter where you are.

It's no longer about Los Angeles, Miami, New York, Chicago, and maybe a few Texas markets. Make no mistake, those places, with large numbers of Latinos to begin with, are posting huge gains, too, in absolute numbers. It's simple math. The Hispanic population in the Los Angeles–Long Beach Primary Metropolitan Statistical Area (PMSA) grew by 28 percent in the 1990s. That's hardly a growth rate to sneeze at. Who wouldn't want their potential customer base to increase by that much over a decade?

In raw numbers, though, it's even more significant. Between 1990 and 2000, the number of Latinos in the L.A. PMSA went up by almost a million. Now, who wouldn't want that kind of growth in their potential market?

The emerging markets, by contrast, may post smaller gains in absolute terms, but because we're generally talking about smaller cities or rural areas to start with, the changes are even more dramatic in terms of their impact.

In December 2005, a U.S. Department of Agriculture

bulletin noted that "Hispanic population growth has helped to stem decades of small-town population decline in some states, *demographically and economically revitalizing many rural communities.*"

I added the emphasis to make a point: "economically revitalizing" is code for "changing market." It also means "opportunity." What the report is saying is that without the influx of Hispanics, those markets were shrinking. In fact, it says, "All else being equal, over 100 nonmetro [sic] counties would have lost population between 1990 and 2000."

According to the USDA report, the Latino population in rural and small-town America nearly doubled between 1980 and 2000, going from 1.4 million to 2.7 million in non-metro counties. Other points worth thinking about:

- In 2000, for the first time, more than half of all non-metro Hispanics lived outside the Southwest.
- The non-metro Hispanic population more than doubled in twenty states, mostly in the South and Midwest. We're talking places like Nebraska, Iowa, Alabama, and Arkansas.

Those who want to be a part of it need to integrate Latino-targeted efforts into their overall marketing plan for the entire country.

THE NEW SALAD BOWL

It's not just about salsa outselling ketchup. Or Spanish showing up as an option at ATMs in Tacoma, Wash. It's about a rapidly swelling number of people adding to the cultural mix, at rates that make them an increasingly large and noticeable part of the demographic landscape. And, like the Irish and Italian and Jewish immigrants before them, even as Hispanics adapt and adopt American ways, we inject some of our ways into it.

There's a difference now, though.

We're not a melting pot anymore. We're a salad.

In a melting pot, everybody kind of turns into one. They don't just mix in, they blend in. In a salad, you still have your individuality. It stands out. People notice.

As Hispanics add their flavor to the American mix, they are much more visibly holding on to their identity. The tomato is still a tomato. The greens are still the greens. The onions are still onions. The beets are beets. And they're all individuals. They all come together to form this new American salad, yet you can still pick them out.

Past immigrants tended to assimilate. They dropped their native customs and, frequently, language, and replaced them with American culture. Hispanics are much more likely to acculturate. They hold on to their cultural traits, even as they pick some up from the mainstream.

Part of the reason has to do with strong, continuing links

to their homelands. Today's immigrant can hop on a plane or drive across the border and be home in a matter of hours. Low-cost long distance makes it easy to maintain frequent, even daily, contact. And a powerful and pervasive Spanish-language media allows Hispanic immigrants to become a part of the United States without completely severing ties with their culture.

We're even seeing a phenomenon called "retro-accultura-tion," with second-, third-, and fourth-generation Hispanics reconnecting with their heritage.

They're part of Hispanic U.S.A., a whole new cultural landscape evolving in this country, with roots in both the American and Latino traditions. This new demographic phe-nomenon is as distinctly American as American culture itself, yet distinctly Latin as well—and determined to hold on to the Spanish language.

Young U.S.-born Latinos may enjoy English-language rock and hip hop, but like Latin rock and Reggaeton just as much. They want *their* MTV—with Eminem and Daddy Yan-kee, Café Tacuba and OutKast.

Over at Mun2, Telemundo's cable offshoot, they call them YLAs—Young Latin Americans. That network put together a yearlong, three-part study about them. It concluded that YLAs live in a hybrid world, vigorously linked to both their Latin and American sides. YLAs are familiar with *South Park* and salsa, *Napoleon Dynamite* and their mom's *telenovela*.

"They have 1,000 English songs on their iPod and 400 Spanish-language ones. They sing Madonna's songs and Paulina

Rubio's as easily as they do Hoobastank's and Don Omar's," said Flavio Morales, vice president of programming at Mun2.

And, unlike the children of previous waves of immigrants, who were encouraged to abandon their old world ways and words, YLAs maintain a strong connection to their Hispanic culture. They see Spanish as a powerful part of their identity, and they believe strongly in Latino family values such as the importance of working hard and respecting family.

Tuning In

Recently, I was in Lexington, Ky., flipping through the radio dial. I found two Spanish-language radio stations—in Lexington!

Those two may be on the AM dial. And only two may be a far cry from the proliferation of Spanish-language stations on AM *and* FM in L.A., where a recent listing showed that twenty-two of the fifty-nine stations broadcast in Spanish. But listening is believing. What I heard in Lexington is evidence that the Hispanic explosion is happening everywhere in the United States, or will be soon.

Turn on your radio. Tune through the dial. Is there a Spanish radio station? Two? Five?

It's a sign. And, remember, the radio stations come after the audience is already there.

In Atlanta, Clear Channel radio switched station WWVA

from general market programming to a Spanish-language format in late 2004. Instantly, it went from a 1.6 to an 11.3 share among 18- to 34-year-old listeners, according to Arbitron.

The radio network followed with changes at its stations in Washington, D.C., and Orlando. By the time it did, in early 2005, Florida already had displaced New Jersey as home to the second largest concentration of Puerto Ricans in the country (behind New York). Close to half of those in Florida lived in the Orlando area. And they only accounted for about half of all the Hispanics living there.

In September of that year, NextMedia followed suit—in Milwaukee, Wisc.!

It launched 104.7-FM La GranD, the first Spanish-language FM radio station, playing a mix of regional Mexican music, including Rancheras, Norteñas, Grupos, Bandas, and Cumbias.

The news release announcing the switch to a Spanish-language format explained why:

"Milwaukee, the nation's twenty-second largest Hispanic market in the U.S., has witnessed explosive Hispanic population growth. According to the 2000 census, Hispanics or Latinos make up approximately 12 percent of Milwaukee's total population. It is reported that Milwaukee's Hispanic community has grown by more than 100 percent over the past ten years."

CHANNEL SURFING

Television proves the same thing.

As early as the spring of 2002, the Spanish-language television network Univision could crow that its stations in New York, Chicago, and Los Angeles had beaten out all the other stations in their markets—English and Spanish—in a key segment. They were number one among 18- to 34-year-old viewers throughout the day.

What's more, in all three markets, Univision's early evening local news crushed the English-language competition, with more 18- to 34-year-olds tuning in than ABC, CBS, and NBC combined.

Ratings in the same sweeps period crowned Univision's San Francisco Bay Area local news the most-watched among 18- to 49-year-olds there.

And it's not just happening in the major metros.

In February 2004, an Associated Press story out of Raleigh, N.C., had this to say:

"Forget ABC, NBC, and CBS. The big ratings winner these days in the heart of North Carolina is WUVC-TV, a six-month-old Spanish-language station."

The article went on to report that the number of viewers among the highly desirable 18- to 34-year-old male segment "tied WUVC with CBS affiliate WRAL-TV for the number one spot in the demographic, meaning that as many men 18 to 34 were watching the *telenovelas*, or Spanish soap operas, broadcast by WUVC as were watching *Everybody Loves Raymond* or *CSI*: *Crime Scene Investigation* over on WRAL."

Later that same year, in October 2004, a *telenovela* hit a milestone. The final, two-hour episode of *Amarte es mi pecado* delivered more 18- to 49-year-old viewers nationwide than ABC, CBS, FOX, WB, or UPN. Nationwide!

There it was, a Friday night, and all across America more people in one of the key demographics were tuned in to a *telenovela* than any other show.

That was just a beginning. From the day Nielsen Media Research began measuring Univision's viewership, the network

The "Hispanic Smile"

beat both the WB and UPN in every rating period. In the summer of 2006, another *telenovela* topped the ratings. And, in July, Univision again scored an impressive landmark: Its 18- to 34-year-old viewership in prime time beat every network but FOX, for an entire week.

The "Hispanic Smile"

Up through the 1980s, Hispanics tended to cluster in a relatively few places within the United States.

Los Angeles, New York, Chicago, and Miami served as major immigration gateways and magnets for continued growth. Those four, along with a few western and southwestern metros with long-established Latino communities were home to fully half of all the Hispanics in the United States.

A 2002 Brookings Institution report dubbed these major Latino centers the "Hispanic heartland in America."

They still are. Certainly in absolute numbers.

The barrios of Los Angeles County make up the second largest Mexican city in the world. Only Mexico City is larger. U.S. census estimates from 2003 put the population of Los Angeles County residents of Mexican descent at nearly 2.8 million. That's almost the same as the population of Chicago. It's more than Houston's. And that's not all the Hispanics in the county. That's only the ones of Mexican descent. In all, there are 4.4 million Hispanics living there. Count them all—

The "Wide Open Grin"

Mexicans, Dominicans, Argentines, and all the rest—and they would constitute the second largest city in the United States, bigger than any place except New York.

That's a lot of people.

Before 1980, though, if you went outside of those four cities and the stretch through the west and southwest, you'd be hard-pressed to find Hispanics, even harder-pressed to find any sizeable bunch.

That's why we used to describe the spread of the Latino presence in this country as the "Hispanic Smile." If you looked at a map of the United States and connected the sweep of major Hispanic markets from New York, down through Florida, across the southwest states of Texas, New Mexico, and Arizona, and up through California, that's what it looked like, a smile.

Chicago was the exception. Maybe we should have called it a smile with a wink.

Nonetheless, the analogy held up. Latinos lived predominantly in concentrated clusters in just a few states, mostly along the coasts and the border with Mexico.

That made it easy to target marketing. And, if you lived in most of the rest of the nation, Hispanics were off the radar, hardly noticeable and hardly worth noting.

Then came what the news and celebrity magazines called "The Hispanic Boom," with Ricky Martin and "La Vida Loca."

The "Wide Open Grin"

The truth now is that Hispanics have spread out. Growing Latino populations live in Iowa, Oregon, Arkansas, and Georgia. They're booming in Raleigh and Columbus, Memphis and Minneapolis, Omaha, Wichita . . . you name it.

Take the Midwest. The Hispanic population of America's Heartland grew by more than 80 percent in the '90s. By 2000, nearly 9 percent of the nation's Latinos made their home in North Dakota, South Dakota, Nebraska, Kansas, Minnesota, Iowa, Missouri, Wisconsin, Illinois, Michigan, Indiana, and Ohio.

Take a look at that list again: North Dakota? Iowa?

Yes.

THE CHANGE IN THE HISPANIC POPULATION, 1990–2000
TEN FASTEST GROWING STATES

	Number of Hispanics 1990	Number of Hispanics 2000	Change (%)
North Carolina	76,726	378,963	394
Arkansas	19,876	86,866	337
Georgia	108,922	435,227	300
Tennessee	32,741	123,838	278
Nevada	124,419	393,970	217
South Carolina	30,551	95,076	211
Alabama	24,629	75,830	208
Kentucky	21,984	59,939	173
Minnesota	53,884	143,382	166
Nebraska	36,969	94,425	155
United States	22,354,059	35,305,818	58

Source: Pew Hispanic Center tabulations from 1990 and 2000 Census Summary File 1

In 2002, the Brookings Institution identified fifty-one "New Latino Destinations" across the country that "experienced an astonishing and rapid entrance of new Hispanics."

They included places as geographically diverse as Albany and Allentown, Grand Rapids and Louisville, Wilmington and Milwaukee. The smallest rate of increase in any of those places, between 1980 and 2000, was 170 percent.

Tacoma, Wash., and Richmond, Va., saw similar increases. So did Boston and Little Rock, Ark. It went up by 223 percent in Salt Lake City, and nearly twice that in Portland, Oreg.

We could go on. The point is that the "Hispanic Smile" now looks like a wide-open grin, filled-in with Latinos living almost everywhere in the United States.

Most of those places started with relatively small Hispanic populations, to be sure. Even then, though, it adds up. In Springfield, Mass., they counted 24,708 Latinos in 1980. By 2000, they hit 74,227. That's an increase of almost 50,000. During the same period, Springfield's total population only grew by 22,158.

THE CHANGING SOUTH

The Hispanic explosion is reshaping the South.

The Latino population shot up 394 percent in North Carolina between 1990 and 2000, close to quadrupled in Arkansas, Georgia, and Tennessee, while tripling in Alabama, South Carolina, and Kentucky.

In Atlanta alone, the Hispanic population went from 55,000 to 269,000 in that time. And it's not just that there are more in sheer number. Those Hispanics also make up more of the city. As their numbers grew, Latinos went from 2 percent to 7 percent of Atlanta's total population.

As they did, the signs of the Hispanic influx grew increasingly obvious. The Havana Sandwich shop, established in 1976, held a lonely outpost on the changing frontier along the Buford Highway.

By 2002, Peruvian and Salvadoran eateries dished out traditional foods nearby, crowds of young Latinos packed the International Ballroom and the Rex to dance to Caribbean salsa groups and live Mexican music, and Colombian immigrants offered vacation packages at the Frutti Valle travel agency.

Northeast of Atlanta, "Latinization" transformed Dalton, Ga., in just ten years, from the town known as the place where Marla Maples and Deborah Norville came from, into a city where more than 40 percent of the kids in school are Hispanic and the school district has had to recruit teachers from Mexico to serve as a cultural bridge.

In 1990, the census calculated that 6 percent of U.S. residents were Hispanic. Today, one out of every three residents is Latino, and more than sixty mostly Mexican soccer teams play on the city's fields.

The rapid change has converted the "Carpet Capital of the World" into a favorite spot for politicians, reporters, and demographers to visit and point to as an example of the changing South. But it's hardly unique.

They now hold mass in English and Spanish in Morganton, N.C. This factory town is nestled in the same foothills that served as the basis for that 1960s TV vision of perfect rural American paradise, Andy Griffith's Mayberry.

In Shelbyville, Tenn., the "Tennessee Walking Horse Capital of the World," one out of every seven residents is Latino, up from next to none in 1980.

Rogers, Ark., set in the heart of the Ozarks and best known as the home of Sam Walton's very first Wal-Mart, saw a similar surge. In 1994, then-Mayor John Sampler stumbled across a group of Latinos playing soccer on a field right there in town.

As a *Newsweek* article described the encounter:

"It was an astonishing sight for Sampler, 54, who had never before met a Latino. His response: to form Arkansas's first Hispanic soccer league. The players were so thrilled that they invited him to their first awards banquet. When he addressed them in Spanish, they went wild, chanting, *¡Viva el alcalde!'* ('Long live the mayor!')."

In just the five years between 1995 and 2000, 1.2 million Hispanics moved into the South. A full one-third of all U.S. Hispanics now make their homes in the South, more than the Northeast and Midwest combined.

And the effect will be even more dramatic in the future. The school-age Hispanic population, kids from 5 to 17 years old, grew 322 percent in the South in the '90s. The same group of white kids went up just 10 percent; blacks, 18 percent.

Hispanic preschoolers, the 4 and younger crowd, shot up even more, 382 percent, adding nearly three times more kids than non-Hispanic whites in the area.

Hypergrowth Markets

Even such unlikely places as Omaha, Des Moines, and Oklahoma City saw their Latino populations double, triple, and more between 1980 and 2000.

But that was nothing compared to the surges in Minneapolis, Tulsa, Providence, and Portland. There, the influx is not just dramatic, it's staggering.

Across the nation, Robert Suro of The Brookings Institution identified eighteen "hypergrowth" metros that racked up Hispanic population gains of 300 percent or more.

They include the area known as the Triangle, around Raleigh, Durham, and Chapel Hill, where the Latino population shot up a phenomenal 1,180 percent.

The effect extends fifty miles up U.S. 64 from there, to Siler City. The place might sound familiar. It's the real-life town where the fictional folks of Mayberry said they did their Saturday shopping. In 1990, the town's population was about 70 percent white and 30 percent black. By the next census, it had become about 40 percent Hispanic, and parishioners planted jalapeño peppers in the garden at the new adobe-style church, St. Julia's.

But it's not just happening in small towns that started with a minuscule Hispanic population. We already mentioned Atlanta. There, a 995 percent increase built a Latino population with more people than the whole of Anchorage. In Orlando,

"HYPERGROWTH"* NEW LATINO DESTINATIONS, 2000

	Number of Latinos	Percent of Total Population	Latino Growth, 1980–2000
Raleigh	72,580	6%	1180%
Atlanta	268,851	7%	995%
Greensboro	62,210	5%	962%
Charlotte	77,092	5%	932%
Orlando	271,627	17%	859%
Las Vegas	322,038	21%	753%
Nashville	40,139	3%	630%
Fort Lauderdale	271,652	17%	578%
Sarasota	38,682	7%	538%
Portland	142,444	7%	437%
Greenville	26,167	3%	397%
West Palm Beach	140,675	12%	397%
Washington, D.C.	432,003	9%	346%
Indianapolis	42,994	3%	338%
Minneapolis-St. Paul	99,121	3%	331%
Fort Worth	309,851	18%	328%
Providence	93,868	8%	325%
Tulsa	38,570	5%	303%
Total	2,750,564	9%	505%

*Hypergrowth metros had a Latino population growth over 300 percent between 1980 and 2000.

Source: Brookings Institution/Pew Hispanic Center

Fla., within sight of the giant Mickey Mouse's ears marking the entrance of that most-American amusement park, Disney World, Hispanics increased by 859 percent—for a total even bigger than Atlanta's.

These are markets that weren't on the radar screen ten years ago. Now, all of a sudden, they merit two and three radio stations and a television station coming in and providing service for them.

Yes, the top five markets are critical to the growth of your business. But the future is clear. The blueprint is starting to form. What the Houston market was twenty years ago is now the Carolinas.

And it's not the people in Houston moving out. It's new folks coming in.

It adds up.

During the '90s, North Carolina, Arkansas, Georgia, and Tennessee registered four- to six-fold increases. Then, in just the two years between 2000 and 2002, Georgia's Latino population grew by another 17 percent. North Carolina was right behind at 16 percent, followed by Nevada, Kentucky, and South Carolina.

Chain Migration

The first arrivals come for jobs. They might be new immigrants from outside the United States. They might be transplants from another U.S. city.

Soon enough, they spread the word to friends and relatives where they came from. More workers arrive, drawn by employer demand. Mostly it's men who come in this first wave. They find jobs, settle in.

Then they bring their wives and children to join them, and stay. Behind them come more friends and relatives.

The residents of whole towns follow one another. Some 90 percent of the immigrants from Tonatico, a small town 100 miles south of Mexico City, head for Waukegan, Ill., to join the 5,000 already there. People from Puebla head for New York. Ones from Veracruz and Oaxaca head for Raleigh, N.C.

Demographers call it "chain migration." It's something every business owner should know—and be ready to take advantage of.

When the businessman first hears Spanish spoken in his neighborhood, he should start paying attention. That's when the sign should go up that says, "We speak Spanish here."

Because the people speaking Spanish in that neighborhood are calling their friends and relatives back home. There will be more coming.

The business that puts out a welcome mat is going to get their business. And when their friends and relatives arrive, it's likely to get their business, too.

GOING TO MARKET

Small wonder the food industry loves us so much. We're the force behind the growth in supermarket shopping. They're carefully studying the products Hispanics over-index in, and discovering that it might be worthwhile to take a fresh look at the categories that did well when the Baby Boom began.

With large, young families, Hispanics buy more toothpaste, disposable diapers, popcorn, cookies, and birthday cakes, among other things.

"They tend to be larger households, have more kids and a higher growth rate," said Libbey Paul, a senior vice president of marketing at ACNielsen, the marketing information company. "You can understand why Kellogg's would care, why Coke would care." To tap into burgeoning Hispanic populations in their neighborhoods, stores are stocking up on traditional Latino foods as well. They're devoting more shelf space to rice and cheese, and making room for things like *masa harina*, *comales*, and canned chipotles.

Large families also need places to live. After a stint at Univision, former HUD Secretary Cisneros joined with a homebuilder in Texas. He was taking a long-term view.

"What we're finding is it's a huge opportunity because of the rate of household formation," he said. "It's the fastest growth in home ownership of any group in the U.S. Ten million new homes will be formed by the end of the decade, half of those will be minority, and more than half of those will be

Hispanic. That's almost 3 million new homes that can be sold to Latino households." Cisneros sees the Hispanic boom as an opportunity. So do the supermarkets. And the Minnesota bankers. You should, too. The second key is that we're everywhere. But it's up to you to make the connection, and make us your customers.

Ask yourself if you have a product or service that appeals to young adults, or young families. It could be cars or furniture, toys or daycare, DVDs or beer.

Then ask yourself if you include products specifically attractive to Latino consumers. A furniture store might increase sales by offering more cribs and kids' furnishings. Music, book, and movie rental shops should dedicate display space to Spanish-language products.

Every business should include Spanish-language signage and bilingual staff to help customers who don't speak English. Hispanics need auto insurance and mortgages, and will get them from someone they can talk to. Even an English-dominant Latino born and raised in the United States may not recognize *nopalitos* by their English-language name of tender cactus.

Chapter 3

WE LOVE THE U.S.A.

Latinos believe in the American Dream. Forget all the rhetoric, pandering, and panic. Hispanics come to the United States for the same reasons the Founding Fathers did. They come to build a better life. Hispanics love this country more than any other because it offers them the opportunity to make their dreams come true.

It shows up in lots of different ways.

Hero Street

Barely a block-and-a-half long, in a small city west of Chicago, it used to be just Second Street. But this tiny bit of Silvis, Ill., earned its new name with blood and tears.

Over the course of thirty years, it contributed more men to combat than any other similarly sized stretch in the country.

The twenty-two Mexican-American families on this street sent a total of fifty-seven young men to fight in World War II and Korea, another twenty in Vietnam. At least one earned a Silver Star. Eight never came home.

The youngest lied about his age to join the Army Air Corps at 17. He was the first from the street to die, trapped in a burning B–24 shot down over Aviano, Italy, on Jan. 31, 1944.

Just up the street from his home, the Sandovals sent six sons to fight in World War II. Two died, one fighting the Japanese, the other against the Germans.

Another family of Sandovals, unrelated to the first, sent seven to the war. William, who dreamed of becoming a boxer, died in a battle in German-held woods outside Nijmegen, Holland.

Claro Soliz and Peter Masias died in that same war, too, in different battles in different places.

Then came Korea. Two Sandovals went to war again, and came home again. Joe Gomez and Johnny Munos didn't.

Joe died charging alone up a hill to clear the way to save a group of trapped American and U.N. soldiers. His bravery earned him a Silver Star.

Johnny died fighting on another hill three months later, on Aug. 27, 1951.

Those were different times. When their brothers and friends returned from the war, they weren't allowed to join the local VFW.

But Joe Terronez, a determined city councilman, wouldn't

forget. "Those boys could have said, 'I'm going back to Mexico so I don't have to risk my life,'" Terronez said later. "Instead, fifty-seven put their lives on the line for the United States, and eight of them died."

Twenty years after Johnny Munos died, on Memorial Day, 1971, Second Street was officially renamed. At the ceremony, as a *Reader's Digest* article recalled later, officials unveiled a red-white-and-blue sign proclaiming it "Hero Street, U.S.A.," and "the Los Amigos marching band swung into 'America' from *West Side Story*."

Four years later, they paved it.

All Aboard

The men of Hero Street are part of a long tradition.

The guy who shouted, "Damn the torpedoes! Full steam ahead!" during the Civil War was Hispanic. David Farragut went on to become the U.S. Navy's first admiral. His father, Jorge, was born in Minorca, off the coast of Spain. But Jorge joined the Americans to fight against the British in the Revolutionary War. He earned a special thank-you from the governor of South Carolina for his heroism.

There are plenty more. By 2002, the census counted 1.1 million Latino veterans of the U.S. armed forces. They include Guy Gabaldon, an orphan from the streets of L.A. who joined the marines and earned a Navy Cross for single-handedly capturing more than 1,000 enemy Japanese, more than 800 of them in a single night.

In World War I, Nicholas Lucero received the French Croix de Guerre for wiping out two German machine gun nests and maintaining steady fire for three hours. Marcelino Serna got one too, along with the Distinguished Service Cross, the Victory Medal with three bars, and two Purple Hearts for the unaided capture of twenty-four enemy soldiers.

One Texas family gave all it could to the conflicts in Afghanistan and Iraq. Army Cpl. Jose A. Velez died in November 2004 in Fallujah as he helped clear an enemy stronghold, gunned down by hostile fire. He was 23. Two years later, in the summer of 2006, his 22-year-old brother, Army Spc. Andrew Velez, died tracking Osama bin Laden in Afghanistan. They were the only sons Roy Velez had.

"I can't be angry. I feel like my heart's been pulled out," the father said. "We've done what the Lord allowed us to do for our country."

By the time of the war in Iraq, forty-one Latinos had been awarded the Congressional Medal of Honor, the highest honor conferred for military bravery.

It's evidence of our patriotism. Hasbro saw it as an opportunity.

In 2001, the toy maker introduced its first Hispanic G.I. Joe. The 12-inch-tall doll honored Army sergeant Roy P. Benavidez, who earned his Medal of Honor for saving eight Special

Forces soldiers during a fierce jungle firefight in Vietnam in 1968.

Hasbro was hardly the first to recognize that patriotic fervor, and see how it connected to its product line.

As *National Geographic* noted in a 2003 article: "Ten years ago the Eder Flag Manufacturing Company decided to offer the Stars and Stripes in a bilingual wrapper. The results have been overwhelmingly positive. 'Latinos want to fly the flag, too,' says marketing director Jim Kowalewski. 'Even the ones who can't yet speak English are proud of America.'"

Home Sweet Home

Home ownership among Hispanics is growing faster than for any other group in the country—twice as fast as non-Hispanic whites and four times as fast as African-Americans.

We put down roots for a reason: This is home. This is where we want to be. This is the place we love.

Not surprisingly, a banker noticed. In a 2002 speech to members of the North Carolina Bankers Association, John W. Mallard Jr., the president of Cardinal State Bank, said:

"About four years ago, we began to notice a tremendous influx of Hispanic families in our state. Some of my fellow bankers and I realized these newcomers brought with them some great opportunities, opportunities that could potentially impact banking forever."

One of the things he quickly realized was that the new arrivals came, and didn't leave.

"Home ownership is the American Dream," he said, "and I assure you the Hispanic population was drawn here in search of their dreams."

Also, unlike previous waves of immigrants, Mallard noted what demographers are seeing all across the country. Many of these newcomers were heading straight for the suburbs, "in search of better schools and safer streets."

In faraway Reno, Nev., Raquel Martinez is one of them. A single mother of four, she worked steadily at her dream—went to college, sought advice from the Reno Housing Authority, applied for federal grants. Finally, a job promotion gave her what she needed to buy a three-bedroom home in Sun Valley.

"I come from a family that doesn't give up," she told the *Reno Gazette-Journal*. "I wanted to improve. I wanted a house."

Of course, that's good news for banks offering mortgages, furniture companies, and a whole host of other businesses connected to housing, directly or indirectly.

Everybody from Ikea to the corner lamp shop, and Home Depot to the neighborhood hardware store makes money off homebuyers, sooner or later. And, as every homeowner knows, so do plumbers, electricians, and the other repairmen that are inevitably called for help.

RATES OF HOME OWNERSHIP	1996	1997	1998	1999	2000	2001	2002	2003	2004
U.S. total	65.4	65.7	66.3	66.8	67.4	67.8	67.9	68.3	69.0
White, total	69.1	69.3	70.0	70.5	71.1	71.6	71.8	72.1	72.8
White, non-Hispanic	71.7	72.0	72.6	73.2	73.8	74.3	74.5	75.4	76.0
Black, total	44.1	44.8	45.6	46.3	47.2	47.4	47.3	48.1	49.1
Other race	51.0	52.5	53.0	53.7	53.5	54.2	54.7	56.0	58.6
American Indian, Aleut, Eskimo	51.6	51.7	54.3	56.1	56.2	55.4	54.6	54.3	55.6
Asian or Pacific Islander	50.8	52.8	52.6	53.1	52.8	53.9	54.7	56.3	59.8
Hispanic	42.8	43.3	44.7	45.5	46.3	47.3	48.2	46.7	48.1
Non-Hispanic	67.4	67.8	68.3	68.9	69.5	69.9	70.0	70.8	71.5

Source: U.S. Census Bureau. Web

Taking Care of Business

Another reason Hispanics love the U.S.A. is because this really is the land of opportunity, for anyone with an entrepreneurial bent. Latinos included.

About two million Hispanics owned their own businesses in 2004, according to the Small Business Administration. And that's expected to double every five years. In 2004, those businesses generated close to $300 billion in sales.

In a comprehensive national survey, the U.S. Census found that:

- Hispanic businesses grew at more than three times the national average for all businesses—31 percent, compared to 10 percent—between 1997 and 2002.
- Nearly three in ten Hispanic-owned firms operated in construction and other services, such as personal services, and repair and maintenance.
- Firms owned by people of Mexican origin accounted for more than 44 percent of all Hispanic-owned firms.
- Retail and wholesale trade accounted for 36 percent of Hispanic-owned business revenue.
- There were 29,184 Hispanic-owned firms with receipts of $1 million or more.
- There were 1,510 Hispanic-owned firms with 100 employees or more, generating more than $42 billion in gross receipts.

In 1997, when the Census Bureau did its last survey, it counted 1.2 million Latino-owned businesses. Close to 12,000 of them were in Georgia. Three years later, the number had grown by more than 10 percent, to 13,251, and Georgia ranked thirteenth among the states for Hispanic-owned businesses.

Evidence stood out clearly on a mile-long piece of Alpharetta Street in Roswell, metro Atlanta's second largest city. By 2000, it boasted several Latino markets, a Mexican bakery, a Latino bank, and a Hispanic video store.

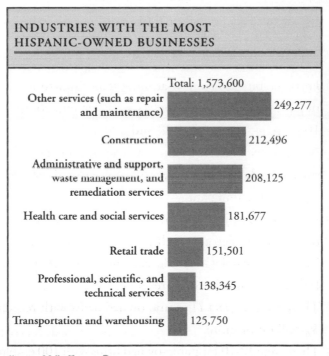

INDUSTRIES WITH THE MOST HISPANIC-OWNED BUSINESSES

Total: 1,573,600

Other services (such as repair and maintenance)	249,277
Construction	212,496
Administrative and support, waste management, and remediation services	208,125
Health care and social services	181,677
Retail trade	151,501
Professional, scientific, and technical services	138,345
Transportation and warehousing	125,750

Source: U.S. Census Bureau
2002 Survey of Business Owners: Hispanic-Owned Firms

That growth doesn't stop at that first tier of mom-and-pops. As far back as 1997, the census reported that 2 percent of Latino businesses had receipts of over $1 million a year.

Before he became a Georgia state senator, Sam Zamarripa teamed up with former investment banker Alex Suarez to launch a business-to-business Internet marketplace linking Hispanic businesses with Fortune 500 companies.

"It's not about today's Internet, it's about tomorrow's America," Suarez told *Georgia Trend* magazine.

The North Carolina Hispanic Chamber of Commerce formed in 1996 with fifteen members. Just over five years later, it had 200.

Luis Rodriguez was a perfect example of why. Arriving in the southern state in 1990, he started as a roofer. He formed his own company. One by one, over the years, he brought ten brothers and cousins from Mexico, trained them, and put them to work.

The moral of the story, from North Carolina banker Mallard: "Just getting a job is not enough for many Latino workers, they want to improve their status."

It's true there. It's true in Colorado.

Linda Torres-Winters grew up in a family of migrant workers. She went to college, married, and moved to Denver. She always liked hiking and got a taste of dehydrated foods on the trail. In the early '90s, she started experimenting and came up with a dry salsa mix. By 1996, most Denver grocery stores carried it, and she was working on a deal with Sam's Club.

Pepe Badia started out mixing spices on a table in his parents' garage, filling bottles by hand with a homemade cardboard funnel, selling to tiny mom-and-pop bodegas on Miami Beach out of the back of his station wagon. That was 1968. By 2004, Badia Spices was busily adding 27,000 square feet to the 65,000 its warehouse and packing plant already had and distributing its line of more than 350 products nationwide. Sales hit $30 million the year before and were climbing easily toward $40 million in '04.

Stories like theirs repeat themselves all across the country every day.

So what?

Wells Fargo Co. gets it. In 1997, the bank did a study that found that access to financing stood as one of the biggest obstacles for Latino business owners. It responded with a goal of lending $1 billion to Hispanic businesses within six years. They hit it in two. The new goal: $3 billion by 2007.

Office Depot gets it, too. The company launched several campaigns aimed at Latinos in 2003 and started a Spanish-language website listing 14,000 items for sale. The chain recognized that Latino-owned businesses are the fastest growing segment, and they need office supplies.

They also need accountants, computer repairmen, vehicles, and a host of other products and services. Who's going to give it to them? You, or your competition?

HISPANIC-OWNED BUSINESSES (ESTIMATED)		
2004	2 million	$300 billion
1997	1.2 million	$114.4 billion
1992	0.9 million	$77 billion

Source: U.S. Census and industry estimates

Let's Go Shopping

There's money being spent, and money to be made.

Vincent Riggio, partner in Plaza Fiesta, a 350,000-square-foot shopping mall in metropolitan Atlanta, sees it every day.

Painstakingly modeled after Latin American village squares in pastels and terra-cotta, the thirty-five stores in Plaza Fiesta are predominantly run for, and by, Hispanics.

The owners who rent space from him, Riggio told *Georgia Trend*, "are no different from your ancestors or mine. They simply want their own business. I have one man who started in a flea market booth and now has 4,500 square feet of space and a $2 million inventory. That's America."

A Shared Dream

President George W. Bush said much the same.

In a meeting with the U.S. Hispanic Chamber of Commerce in 2001, he noted that there were, by then, 600,000 Latino-owned businesses in California alone.

"This is what America is all about," he said, "the idea of somebody having a dream. It doesn't matter what your background is, where you're from. If you work hard and dream big, you can realize your dream."

Inspirational words, words he knew Latinos take to heart.

"I used to tell the folks in my great state of Texas," he went on, "I said, 'I welcome the Hispanic influence in our state. It makes Texas a richer place, a stronger place, a place that I'm proud to call home.' And that's the way I feel about America, too."

Our Walter Cronkite

Opportunity comes in different forms.

Born in Mexico, Jorge Ramos is the most popular Spanish-language anchor in the United States, an internationally recognized and influential journalist, syndicated newspaper columnist, and respected author of six books in English and Spanish.

He has covered five wars and won seven Emmys, including the first two ever given to a Spanish-language newscast in the United States.

Over the years, he has interviewed George W. Bush, Bill Clinton, Al Gore, George H.W. Bush, John Kerry, John Edwards, Fidel Castro, Vicente Fox, and Carlos Salinas de Gortari.

The *Wall Street Journal* called him "Hispanic TV's number one correspondent and key to a huge voting bloc." The research firm Hispanic Trends described him as "one of the most influential Latinos" in the United States.

Basically, he's our modern-day Walter Cronkite. *En español.*

Ramos grew up in Mexico. He left after the biggest Mexican television network censored one of his news reports. At the time, Mexico lived under an authoritarian government. Many journalists took bribes and accepted censorship as a fact of life. Ramos didn't. He headed north. He came to the United States on a student visa in 1983. His first job was as a waiter. He was twenty-five. Three years later he became one of the youngest national news anchors in U.S. history.

Ramos clings proudly to his heritage. But now, he says, "When I am in the United States, I am the Mexican. But when I go back to Mexico, I am the American. . . . I feel this sense of pride and allegiance to both Mexico and the United States. No question, the United States has given me many more opportunities than *Méjico*. And for that," he adds, his voice cracking with emotion, "I love this country."

There's another reason Latinos love the United States so much. It has to do with what we cover in Chapter Five, our strong family values. We passionately want a better life for our children.

It's a reason Ramos knows personally.

"I have to be very honest and realistic," he says. "I believe that my children will have a better life than me, simply because they were born in the United States. If my children had been born in any other country, I'm not sure I would have been able to say that. But because they were born here, I am completely sure that they will have a better life than the one I had."

Field of Dreams

Raymond Moreno says: "Here there's no caste system, and it's easier to succeed."

As a child, Moreno worked side-by-side with his parents, picking vegetables. One year, with a frost fast approaching and the farm's owner urging the field laborers on, Moreno found himself picking tomatoes as fast as he could. Moreno, a ninth grader, snapped. He swore to change his life. The solution: education. Moreno went to school, became a physician.

"I always knew I'd find a way out of those fields," he says. Yolanda and Rogelio Garcia stand as similar proof of our belief in the value of education.

They work 365 days a year, often starting after midnight

and working fourteen hours straight. Every day, rain or shine, they steer their old white truck through the back alleys of Los Angeles neighborhoods—gathering cans to pay for their children's college educations.

For more than a decade, the couple steadily collected some 45,000 cans a month, earning them, on average, between $1,400 and $1,600. They won't accept welfare. And they don't waste a penny. What doesn't go toward food, gas, and rent goes to their 19-year-old daughter, Adriana, at UC Riverside, and to Rogelio Jr., studying aeronautical engineering at MIT.

They're evidence of what Linda Robinson wrote in a 1998 article in *U.S. News*: "Half of Southern California's native Latino families, and one third of those from abroad, are middle class. New arrivals often hold two jobs, leveraging themselves or their children into such middle-income occupations as police officer, manager, and executive secretary."

Some of the better-known Latinos who prove her point include Eduardo Sanchez, co-director of *The Blair Witch Project*, and Robert Rodriguez, director of *El Mariachi* and *Spy Kids*.

George Reyes became Google's chief financial officer in 2002, after thirteen years at Sun Microsystems. And Jim Padilla, Ford Motor Company's president and COO, stepped down in 2006 after forty years with the car maker.

Many successful Hispanics are showing their love for the country that gave them the chance to make their dreams come true by giving something back, through public service and benevolent initiatives.

Carlos Gutierrez, who fled Fidel Castro's Cuba for Miami Beach when he was 6, worked his way up from sales rep selling Frosted Flakes in Mexico City to CEO of Kellogg's. Then, in 2004, he gave up a $7.4 million compensation package to become the U.S. Commerce Secretary—giving him responsibility for overseeing the Census Bureau's measurement of demographic trends and data.

That same year, former Texas Supreme Court justice and White House counsel Alberto Gonzales took over as U.S. Attorney General. As he stepped down, another Hispanic cabinet member stepped down to run for the Senate. Mel Martinez won his race in Florida, becoming one of the nation's two Latino senators.

When Hector Ruiz took over as chairman and CEO of computer-chipmaker AMD in 2002 he delivered a message to the company's workers setting a visionary goal based on his own life experience.

"As a child growing up in Mexico," he said, "I became aware at an early age of the importance of education. As I have learned and developed in my career, I have discovered that perhaps no force can have a greater impact on promoting education than technology." The goal: "to empower 50 percent of the world's population with affordable access to the Internet by 2015."

Bringing It Home

So what do all those stories mean? Hispanics are here to stay. We believe in the U.S.A., and we want to be a part of it.

As we said at the beginning of this chapter: Latinos come here for the same reasons the Founding Fathers did, to build a better life. And we want every generation to do better than the one before. We want to participate and contribute at every level—economically, culturally, and politically. We want to own homes, build businesses, and, when we can, we want to give something back to show our gratitude.

That's an opportunity for anyone who sells products or services small (and, more and more, large) businesses need.

If you're an accounting firm, do you have Spanish speakers on staff? The owner of an electrical contracting firm may know everything he needs to know about wires, conduits, and running his business, but still feel his English is weak. He's going to prefer doing business with someone he's comfortable talking to, whether he's looking for an accountant, a tax preparer, a banker, or an insurance agent.

Everyone related to the housing industry should recognize that Hispanics are the fastest growing segment of the home-buying market. Owning a home is a fundamental part of the American Dream, and that's what we're after. We want to put down roots.

That's worth keeping in mind, no matter what business you're in.

One result of that is, we're going where the homes are: Hispanics are heading to the suburbs, bringing the biggest demographic shift since the period right after World War II. Businesses in those areas that put out the welcome mat—with store signs in Spanish, or by including products we like—give themselves an advantage.

Hispanic home owners need roofs and decorations, furniture and security alarms. They need pool chemicals and kitchen appliances, barbecues and bed sheets. In short, we need everything every other home owner does. But we're more likely to buy from someone who shows they understand us and takes our tastes into account.

What do I mean? Latinos like to decorate their houses with crosses and mirrors. If you sell household ornaments, have you included those things in your stock? How about painted ceramic or terra-cotta pots, planters, vases, and pitchers? We like those, too.

Homebuilders hoping to attract us should keep certain characteristics in mind. Most Hispanics are younger than the general market. With an average age of around 27, that means more young couples and more young families fitting in the "starter home" category.

But because families tend to stick together to help each other out, many of those may already be bringing Grandma or other extended family members to live with them. We also tend to have more kids than the general market, and to have them when we're younger. That means we may need more room, or at least be thinking about the day when we will need more room. Offering "starters" with a spare room or "room to grow" can be a smart strategy.

You could gain a competitive advantage by thinking about the needs of multiple generations when you plan your neighborhood amenities, such as clubhouses and recreation and community centers. Young moms and dads jogging together as they push baby in a running stroller might look good in ads, but the reality is it may be Grandma who'll be taking baby for most of her walks. She might prefer lots of shade and a place to sit and chat with friends to a Vita course.

And don't forget the importance of food in Latino culture. Much of our family life, from entertaining to family gatherings, centers around meals and cooking. Offering bigger kitchens, with room for more family members, can be a draw your competition hasn't thought of.

Chapter 4

WE VOTE

George W. Bush gets it. He understands the power and value of the Hispanic vote. It got him elected, not once, but four times—twice as governor of Texas, twice as president.

What he recognized matters. To you. And you can put it to work for you whether you're a politician or a plumber.

We'll explain.

Lone Star Lessons

Bush learned early that you need Latinos to win.

The first time he ran for Texas governor, he campaigned intensely for their vote. It paid off. He whittled away just enough of popular Democratic governor Ann Richards' Hispanic support to win. Barely. Bush got less than 30 percent of the Latino votes cast—somewhere between 24 and 29 percent depending on the poll—but that was enough. It helped push him over the top.

It was significant. But it was only a starting point.

"The victories will be nothing more than a flash in the pan unless Republicans reach out to Hispanics," former Texas governor Bill Clements wrote in an open letter to his party. "Hispanics must have an important role in the future of the Texas Republican Party. If they don't, when people discuss minorities in the years ahead, they won't be talking about Hispanics. They'll be referring to Texas Republicans."

The second time around, in 1998, Bush made history —twice over. He became the first Texas governor to win reelection in a quarter of a century. He also became the Lone Star State's first Republican gubernatorial candidate ever to win the heavily Hispanic and Democratic border counties of El Paso, Cameron, and Hidalgo. He deliberately went after the Latino vote, and got it. Bush pulled better than 40 percent of the Hispanic vote—unprecedented for a Republican—and crushed his competition.

Going National

Republican Party consultant Lance Tarrance recognized the impact of what Bush accomplished in Texas and, more importantly, its significance. Tarrance helped engineer the successful "Southern strategy" that wrested the South from the hands of the Democrats and turned it into a Republican stronghold. In January 2000, with the campaign to regain control of the White House in full swing, Tarrance told the annual gathering of the Republican National Committee that the party's future demanded a new strategy. "For the last three decades, we've had a Southern strategy," he said. "The next goal is to move to a Hispanic strategy for the next three decades."

He didn't have to tell George Bush. Months earlier, in advance of the Iowa Caucus, Team Bush was already targeting Hispanics there with a sixty-second Spanish-language radio spot. In Iowa! America's Heartland!

"Once again, the spotlight is on Iowa. And for the first time it's shining on the Latino community," the ad said. "We're voters, too, and George W. Bush believes that all Iowans should help elect a president. . . . In this presidential election you will see a fresh start, the beginning of a new day for Latinos."

The Texas governor put together a campaign team that practically flooded the Spanish-language media with translated news releases, audio, and video clips. They offered interview opportunities, in Spanish, with the candidate or his fully fluent proxies. Bush's Spanish had its limits, and he admitted he could mangle the language in his effort to communicate, but—and this is something every business owner could learn from him—his attempts endeared him to Hispanics. In fact, three years later, a Tomás Rivera Policy Institute survey of 1,232 television viewers in Los Angeles, Houston, and New York proved it.

"Many bilingual Latino viewers respond to candidates and elected officials who make the effort to speak to them in Spanish," report author Louis DeSipio concluded. "Such an effort only matters to about half of respondents, but for those [to whom] it does matter, there is an overwhelmingly positive reaction. Clearly, candidates and office holders need to speak also to the substantive needs of Latinos, but language can offer a tool to make an initial connection."

A year later, a joint *Washington Post*, Univision, and Tomás Rivera Policy Institute survey reconfirmed the finding. It asked 1,605 Latinos across the country how important it was for a candidate to speak to them in Spanish. More than four out of ten (42 percent) said it was very important. Another 23 percent called it somewhat important. Of the rest, 16 percent answered that it was somewhat unimportant. Less than one in five, 18 percent, said it was not at all important.

Bottom line: We like you for trying.

BRINGING IT HOME

Bush connected with Hispanics on themes we identify with: family values, the economy, and education. And he made sure Latinos knew it.

Bush made history in the 2000 campaign, when he ran

Spanish-language TV ads during the primary. It was a first for a Republican presidential candidate. The ad keyed on motifs of tradition, family, and patriotism.

But while we share those beliefs, we want more.

"The three most important issues for Hispanics are getting a college education for their children, buying a home, and earning enough money to share with other members of their family," Tarrance told the online magazine *Salon*. "Now, is there any other ethnic group that you can say that about?

The Hispanic registered voters in the Pew survey said the things they considered most important overall were:

- Education (54%)
- The economy and jobs (51%)
- Health care and Medicare (51%)
- U.S. campaign against terrorism (45%)
- The war in Iraq (40%)
- Crime (40%)
- Social Security (39%)
- Moral Values (36%)
- Taxes (33%)
- The federal budget deficit (30%)
- Immigration (27%)

Source: Pew Hispanic Center and the Henry J. Kaiser Family Foundation, "The 2004 National Survey of Latinos: Politics and Civic Participation"

Hispanics want the American dream, and they see opportunity through the eyes of their children."

A 2004 Pew Foundation survey reinforced the Republican beliefs about Hispanics. The issues Hispanics care about tend to be pretty much the same ones everyone else cares about.

Just like most folks, Latino parents lose sleep over the education their kids are getting. All of us worry about money, jobs, and the economy. And we sweat over the rising cost of health care, how much our health insurance takes out of our paycheck, and about how many people don't have any at all.

As the chart shows, education and the economy come first among our concerns.

How we feel about these things means more to us than whether a candidate is Latino or not.

Bush knew it. He focused on those Hispanic concerns throughout his 2000 campaign. He may have spoken about tax cuts in New Hampshire. But in Latino strongholds like California, the topic was education.

He unveiled his education plan and $5 billion literacy program in Los Angeles seated next to Jaime Escalante, the former teacher portrayed by Edward James Olmos in the movie *Stand and Deliver*. He spoke about access to college for Hispanics and about "No Child Left Behind."

He called his English literacy proposal *Inglés y más*, English and more, and told a gathering of the Latin Business Association it signified "*todos nosotros, pero juntos.*" All of us, but together.

"I am here with you today," he said, "because you are leaders and because you embody the permanent hope, the durable dream of this nation: to build a better life for ourselves and our children."

It paid off. In the razor-thin 2000 presidential election, the Hispanic vote was vital to Bush's victory.

Estimates based on exit polls have shown him winning as much as 44 percent of the Latino vote across the nation. That's stunning, considering only 20 percent of Hispanics call themselves Republicans.

And surely it was enough to make a critical difference in key "battleground" states like Florida, Arizona, Colorado, and Nevada. Bush took them all. In Florida, Latinos gave Bush a 151,000-vote margin over Al Gore. It mattered. He won the state by a mere 537 votes.

Meeting with Hispanic leaders at the White House shortly after the 2000 election, Bush told them, *"Mi casa blanca es su casa blanca."* My White House is your White House.

Tick Talking

Politicians are extremely attuned to what makes us tick, and what our hot buttons are.

Rule #1: Latinos don't necessarily vote for a Latino candidate. We vote based on what matters to us. And we don't necessarily stick to party lines.

George W. Bush proved it in Texas, where the majority of the Hispanic voters are Democrats. He did it again on the national level, where Democrats continue to hold an advantage among Latinos. Bob Graham, the former U.S. senator from Florida and a steadfast Democrat, drew overwhelming support from staunchly Republican Hispanic voters in election after election.

Issues and qualifications are what are important. Given the same positions on the issues and the same qualifications, most Hispanics would vote for a Latino. But put a better-qualified candidate in the race and he or she wins, no question.

When the Pew Foundation asked the question in a 2004 survey, it found nearly six out of ten registered voters would go for a Latino of equal caliber, but almost three-fourths said they would vote for the best person, no matter what.

The same will hold true for your product or service. You don't have to be Hispanic to sell to us. Give us price and quality. We may choose Badia spices over McCormick's, but not solely because a Hispanic makes them. Pepe Badia knows older Latino women prefer to buy spices in a small cellophane bag, so he packages some small quantities that way. The bilingual labeling on all of his packaging helps. The quality, we expect, is about the same, but Badia spices generally sell for less. In the end, Badia gets our business because he knows what's important to us, not because he's Latino.

REACHING OUT

Bush also understood another key fact about Hispanics: Their ties to their country of origin influence their decisions here.

Bush's top Spanish-language media advisor, Sonia Colín, made it a point to make him available for interviews with the Latin American press. The people there may not be able to vote, she argued, but a potential voter's grandmother or brother-in-law might say they heard Bush speaking Spanish. Favorable comments from family back home could win a few votes here.

That's important for any business. Investing the time, effort, and, yes, money if need be, to build a positive image overseas can have a significant reflected impact here. If relatives over there think well of your brand—if they've had good experiences with their Ford truck, like the taste of Nestle Quik, or have never had a problem with Pampers leaking—that word-of-mouth can mean increased sales here.

Making It Count

Bush knew: Hispanics can make the difference, and he deliberately targeted them. So did Al Gore.

Both spoke Spanish at rallies. Both built Spanish-language websites and advertising campaigns. And both spent an unprecedented amount on Spanish-language television advertising. But Gore's efforts paled by comparison.

Gore sprinkled Spanish into his speeches and appearances on Spanish-language media. But, while Bush tried to converse in the language, Gore's efforts were limited to repeating a few simple slogans.

And Bush outspent Gore in Spanish-language media two to one. Adam J. Segal, of the Hispanic Voter Project at Johns Hopkins University, calculated that the Bush campaign and the Republican National Committee spent $2,274,000 on Spanish-language TV ads. Gore and the Democrats spent just $960,000. Overall, Gore's Spanish-language campaigning seemed like a token effort, and it failed.

The lesson: Half-hearted efforts don't work.

And Bush had another valuable lesson for us: He didn't stop wooing Latinos once he got elected. Bush worked to solidify his gains. He knew that relationships matter to us. We're not just voters or customers, we're friends. Bush held *Cinco de mayo* celebrations at the White House and became the first commander-in-chief to host a weekly radio address in Spanish.

In the 2004 campaign, Bush repeated his Spanish-language strategies. He spent about $5.5 million on ads aimed at Latino voters, keying on the themes of education and aspiration. The ads showed college students graduating and well-heeled Hispanic families laughing. *Nos conocemos*, the ads declared. We know each other.

> **The payoff:** He won again, with an even wider margin of the Hispanic vote. Gore had won New Mexico in 2000. In 2004, Bush did, by less than 6,000 votes, thanks to his surge in Latino support.

Here, There, and Everywhere

It's not just national elections. All across the nation, the number of Hispanic voters is growing enough to provide candidates with the margin they need for victory. Ask Sen. Harry Reid of Nevada.

During his extremely tight 1998 race, state Democrats put out a lot of effort and mobilized 8,000 Latinos to vote, nearly double the number from the previous election. To win them over, Reid turned to his friend, boxing promoter Hank Arum. Arum convinced Oscar De la Hoya to help.

Reid remains convinced the popular boxer's influence with Hispanics made the difference that put him over the top. De la Hoya appeared in Spanish-language campaign ads, at a public rally and at fund-raisers for Reid.

In the end, Reid won by a mere 428 votes, out of more than 400,000 cast.

"He's the reason I'm in the Senate now," Reid told *Newsweek* the following year.

Tower-ing in Texas

The late Sen. John Tower was one of the first to understand this and use it to his political advantage. In fact, the non-Hispanic Texas senator actually understood it better than the Latino he hired to run the advertising for his campaign.

Lionel Sosa went on to become a legendary Hispanic adman and a key player in six presidential campaigns. But as he describes it, when Tower first came to him, he was a partner in a firm that did no Spanish-language advertising. Tower opened his eyes. He showed him the potential, and significance, of courting Latinos.

Lionel is a dear friend who laughs as he tells the story today, of hitting the ice houses in South Texas to sip cold beer at the outdoor picnic tables and meet, greet, listen to, and woo regular, hardworking Hispanic voters.

Tower won by a hair, half of 1 percent, just 12,227 votes over his opponent. Latinos gave him the winning edge. Tower pulled in 37 percent of the Hispanic vote, a 29-point leap over the best any Republican had ever done in Texas.

"Here's a guy who saw it before me," Sosa said.

What Reagan Knew

The experience with Tower led Sosa to split from his partners and focus on Spanish-language and Hispanic-focused campaigns. His partners didn't get it. Sosa did. But, even so, it was another non-Hispanic who taught him more about the keys to understanding Latinos.

Ronald Reagan invited Lionel to create the Spanish-language messages for his ad campaign. When they met, Lionel says, Reagan gave Lionel the strategy, "The key is conservative values—that's what the bond between Latinos and Republicans is—do the commercials on that!"

In one of his more famous quotes, Reagan said, "Hispanics are Republicans; they just don't know it."

What he meant, Reagan said, was that both Hispanics and Republicans believed in the value of family, faith in God, and that America is the greatest country. Those shared values gave them a common connection. Both sides just needed someone to point that out.

By 2004, Reagan's insight was ingrained with his party. Republicans found strong support among evangelical Hispanics just like they did with evangelical non-Hispanics. And, as we'll go on to talk about in the next chapter, family values are a hot button with Latinos.

Since that meeting with Reagan, Lionel has played a crucial role in five more presidential campaigns. He never forgot what Ronald Reagan, the "Great Communicator," taught him.

Willie's War

One of the reasons for the political success, and clout, of Hispanics is directly attributable to a giant among Latinos, Willie Velasquez. What Cesar Chavez was to the farm workers, Willie Velasquez was to Hispanic voters.

Growing up in San Antonio's Mexican-American Westside in the turbulent '60s, Velasquez seized upon the vision that disenfranchised Latinos could win a place in the nation's political process with their vote. His rallying cry became, "*su voto es su voz*"—your vote is your voice.

At the time, it was an oddly novel idea. Hispanics weren't even counted in the census then. Despite their centuries-old presence in the United States, Latinos remained marginalized.

Velasquez founded the Southwest Voter Registration Education Project in 1974, with the simple but powerful goal of convincing Hispanics to sign up and exercise their right to vote. Between 1974 and his untimely death from kidney cancer in 1988, the project registered millions; it won court judgments against gerrymandering and the at-large voting districts that diluted the voting strength of Latinos and other minorities.

Just before Velasquez died, I took over my second television station in San Antonio and once again got involved civically. We met in the last year of Willie's life. I insisted on honoring him by televising his funeral mass held at the great San Fernando Cathedral. The ceremony was presided by the then Bishop of San Antonio, Archbishop Flores, and the rector of the Cathedral, Father Virgil Elizondo. It was a very special day.

He was a true, true inspiration. He's just one of those individuals who should never be forgotten.

Velasquez died three days before he was supposed to introduce Michael Dukakis at the 1988 Democratic convention. He was 44.

"Willie died too young. . . . But in his vibrant life, he restored faith in our ideals and ourselves," President Clinton said when he awarded Velasquez the Medal of Freedom posthumously, the nation's highest civilian honor, in 1995.

Wilson's Folly

Willie Velasquez's efforts opened the way for Latinos to gain the political power they now have. Another reason—and a valuable lesson—comes from someone who wanted to take away that power.

In his 1994 run for office, former California governor Pete Wilson strongly supported the state's controversial Proposition 187. The ballot initiative aimed at cutting off social services for undocumented immigrants. Both Wilson and 187 won by hefty margins. But the backlash brought a stunning increase in Hispanic voter registration.

In the next election, 700,000 more Latinos voted than did just two years before. A full 31 percent of the Latinos who voted in 1996 were first-time voters.

Sergio Bendixen, who has been polling the Latino Electorate for decades—and in my estimation is the best there is—says it well. "It was a defining moment in Latino politics. Wilson did what hundreds of activists had not been able to accomplish. He single-handedly galvanized the Latino voter movement."

In a survey, the new voters told the National Association of Latino Educated and Appointed Officials (NALEO) they became citizens and registered to vote to fight against discrimination. They wanted a voice. They got it.

IMMIGRATION

Today, Latinos have a new voting mission. The congressional debate over U.S. immigration policy united Hispanics, motivated them to take to the streets, and, once again, roused them to register to vote in droves.

The issue also threatens to undo the gains Republicans have had in wooing the Latino vote and push Hispanics back into the Democratic fold. As Sen. Mel Martinez told the *Washington Post*'s David Broder: "We can throw away all that we've gained if we follow a Pete Wilson-style strategy."

In a stunning display of solidarity, millions turned out in cities across the nation last year to protest anti-immigration legislation winding its way through Congress. An estimated 500,000 Latino demonstrators swept through the streets of downtown Los Angeles, a massive sea of flag-waving marchers twenty-six blocks long; so many that it took six hours for the procession to make its way through the city.

In Chicago, there were 300,000. Hundreds of thousands more turned out in Milwaukee, Denver, Phoenix, Tucson, Atlanta, and Reno.

Morning radio show host Eduardo Sotelo, known on the air as *El Piolín*, or "tweety bird," came up with the idea for the demonstrators to turn out in white clothing—for peace and effect. Syndicated in twenty cities, he called on them to carry American flags to show their love of the United States. He convinced eleven fellow radio personalities in L.A. to promote the protest on the airwaves. In addition, ten prime-time Spanish-language television news anchors filmed a promotional spot urging the demonstrators to show respect.

They came to make their feelings known about immigration. But as they marched, many carried signs pointing to the issue's future impact: *Hoy marchamos, mañana votamos.* Today we march, tomorrow we vote.

"The marches made us visible," Renán Almendárez Coello, the Spanish radio disc jockey known as *El Cucuy*, told *USA Today*. "Now, with the vote, we make ourselves present." In the summer after the protests, the Pew Hispanic Center released a new study that showed Latinos felt united by the demonstrations and that a majority of them "believe that the immigration debate will drive more Hispanics to vote and that the marches signal the rise of a new and lasting movement."

It also showed Martinez's fears might be well founded.

"The survey shows that Latinos to some extent are holding the Republican Party responsible for what they perceive to be the negative consequences of the immigration debate, but the political impact of that perception is uncertain," it said.

The possibility is not lost on the Democrats, or on Latino leaders who see disgruntled Hispanics as potential voters ripe for registration. They saw a sudden spike in citizenship applications, up almost 20 percent in 2006 over 2005, as reminiscent of the anti-Wilson backlash in California.

Governor Arnold

Conventional wisdom would have given the vast majority of the overwhelmingly Democratic Hispanic vote in California to the Latino candidate for governor, Cruz Bustamante. But, in Sosa's view, Bustamante, a Democrat, made a mistake. He pushed the "we're victims, in need of government help" theme.

Arnold Schwarzenegger, however, represented an immigrant's American Dream: a foreigner, arriving with nothing, works his way up to become one of the most successful actors in Hollywood, then runs for governor of the most populous state in the Union.

"Latinos love stories like that," Sosa says.

Apparently Bustamante pulled a slim majority among Latinos, 51 percent. But almost a third went with Schwarzenegger. The result: The movie star hauled in almost a million and a half more votes than Bustamante—equal to half again what the Latino candidate got in total.

Loretta Who?

In 1996, practically the opposite happened: A virtually unknown Latina businesswoman in Orange County, Loretta Sanchez, won a stunning upset over ten-time incumbent congressman Bob Dornan.

Dornan had missed the cues. He didn't notice that the electorate in his home base had changed. The margin was razor-thin, fewer than 1,000 votes, but no fluke. When Dornan challenged Sanchez again two years later, Sanchez won again, this time by close to 12,000 votes.

The lesson is worth noting, all across the country. Hispanics aren't just making a difference with their vote. They're running for—and winning—seats on city councils and school boards, county commissions, and in state legislatures. Not just in California, but in Camden, N.J., and Chattanooga, Tenn. It's happening in Kentucky and Kansas, Idaho and Illinois.

By the time they do, chances are that a Latino voting base is already there. The question is: If your business is there, did you notice? Or did your competition?

Rock the Vote

More than 10 million Hispanics registered to vote in 2004. An estimated 8 million voted. Bendixen believes those numbers will double by 2020.

He goes on to say that in '08, it will be the Latino vote that will determine who will be the next president of the United States.

In 1996, 6.5 million Hispanics registered; 5 million cast a ballot. By 2000, registration had risen to 7.5 million. About 6 million voted. In 2008, 10 million are expected to vote.

In some places, such as California and Arizona, the number of Latino voters doubled during the '90s. And there are more on the way. About one-third of the Hispanic population is still too young to vote. And only a third of all Latinos are registered, compared with 61 percent for blacks and 67 percent for whites.

IT MATTERS TO YOU

The way Hispanics vote, and their reasons for voting the way they did, affect everyone.

In part, it's simple civics. The people Latinos help elect, pass laws, and make decisions that everyone must abide by, not just Hispanics. Whether it's a local councilwoman approving a subdivision, a state representative opposing money for a new road, or a U.S. senator pushing for tax reform, the decisions touch more than just the people who voted them in.

But with Hispanics, there's more.

MAKING THE CONNECTION

Latinos believe in a very personal relationship with their elected officials.

Politicians know and are close to the Hispanic business leaders in their communities.

They talk. They see each other.

That's a way for you to gain access to Latino leaders in your area. Get to know the politicians, and they will talk to people in the community about you. You can, effectively, turn your elected official with all due respect, into your assistant marketing manager, promoting your product or service to influential decision makers in the Latino community, and opening doors for new business.

Hispanics place a lot of stock in word-of-mouth. When someone we respect speaks, we listen. And, naturally, the more we respect them, the more we value their opinion. Those we see as successful, like elected officials, fit in that category.

Felipe Korzenny, co-founder of Cheskin, a California-based market research firm, put it this way:

"The recommendations of others who are trustworthy are greatly valued and accepted. That is why neighbors and friends open their doors and their wallets to others they trust."

Companies that rely on friendships and personal introductions to connect with customers—the Avons, Mary Kays, Shaklees, and Tupperwares of the world—are naturals for the Hispanic market.

"These companies," Korzenny wrote, "have experienced exploding growth because they have learned to capitalize on the strong tendency of the market to spread influence and information interpersonally."

Mr. Salazar Goes to Washington

Today, there are nearly 5,000 Hispanic elected officials in the United States, from city council members up. For the first time in nearly thirty years, three Hispanics hold the office of U.S. Senator. One is from Colorado, one from Florida, and one from New Jersey; two are Democrats, one is a Republican.

A record twenty-five Hispanics began U.S. congressional terms following the 2004 elections. NALEO counted more than 230 Latinos elected to state legislatures in thirty-three states.

In addition, President Bush has appointed Hispanics to key cabinet positions. He named former Texas Supreme Court

Justice Alberto Gonzales attorney general, and former Kellogg's CEO Carlos Gutierrez as commerce secretary.

Then, in a bitterly fought runoff election in May 2005, Los Angeles got its first Latino mayor in more than 130 years. Antonio Villaraigosa, a city councilman and former state assembly speaker, won by a wide margin.

Who can say what's next?

We already had a Hispanic president—on *The West Wing*. Martin Sheen, born Ramon Estevez, played President Jed Bartlet on the immensely popular television show. Somewhere in the next two to three presidents we're very likely to see a real-life Hispanic vice presidential candidate.

THE WHOLE ENCHILADA

The meaning of all of this is clear: We vote, and that's significant to more than just politicians. The people who understand can use it to their advantage.

We can learn an awful lot from politicians like George W. Bush. He recognized that Latinos can give you the winning edge. That's true for your business, too.

He proved that you don't have to speak Spanish well to win us over. If your effort seems sincere, we'll like you just for trying. He had us at *¡Hola!*

And you don't have to be Hispanic to get our business. If you give us what we're looking for, and show us you understand our wants and needs, we're yours.

But as Al Gore showed us, half-hearted efforts and taking us for granted can be costly.

The two things that are most important to us are education and the economy. Again, Bush's campaign ads serve as textbook examples of how to make that work for you. He showed images of successful Hispanics—well-off families and kids graduating from college. It was easy for his target audience to make the connection between him and success.

Can aspirational themes establish your product or service as something that will help Latinos make their dreams come true? If you're selling a computer, it might sell better in the general market if you show people all the fun they can have with it. For Hispanics, you might be better off showing how it can help a student improve his grades.

Knowing the value we place on education, your company might consider offering a scholarship, providing tutors, or donating supplies and equipment to classes in Latino neighborhoods. Imagine how much good will you can gain by giving toys, bikes, a laptop, or store gift certificates to the Hispanic child with the best grades in a class your company sponsors.

In a study of Hispanic grocery store shoppers in Los Angeles, New York, Houston, and Miami, Unilever concluded that community activities were one of the top ten satisfaction drivers. It suggested:

- Let your Hispanic customers share their food savvy with the community—organize cooking competitions built around favorite Hispanic dishes.
- Offer health education and basic screenings in the pharmacy area on selected days.
- Participate in neighborhood festivals (offer Hispanic ready-to-eat treats at food fairs).
- Sponsor local youth athletic teams, complete with uniforms displaying your store logo; offer special discounts for youth league post-game snacks and beverages.
- Dedicate a percentage of purchases toward a scholarship fund in your company's name at local community colleges.
- Tie into the Hispanic community's favorite leisure activities—for example, host a monthly dominoes tournament.

Remember, when you're dealing with Hispanics, the sale doesn't end when the cash register closes. As Bush showed us, relationships matter. Business comes out of our continued association. What does that mean? Keep the contact alive. Send greeting cards. No matter what you're selling, don't wait for your customers to come to you, stop by and say hello.

Those personal relationships help build word-of-mouth advertising for you. And nothing is worth more than that. The opinions of people we trust have a powerful influence over our decisions. It can be our neighbor, a relative, or a local political leader. And, as the old commercial said, "They tell two friends. And they tell two friends. And so on. And so on . . . "

Chapter 5

WE HAVE STRONG FAMILY VALUES

It may sound cliché, but family truly comes first for Latinos. It shapes the way we look at the world, and the way we look at ourselves. It shapes our decisions.

It's not unusual for a Latino sales manager to pass up a promotion if it requires moving away from family to another town. As Roberto Villareal of the University of Texas at El Paso put it, there's more "devotion to family and community than to American-style individualism. As an example, one of my top students turned down money from Harvard to stay at UTEP so she could look after her mother."

Study after study has shown what any of us could have told you: Strong family ties go beyond being something important to us. They're part of how we define ourselves as Hispanics. Most of us would rather spend time at home with our family than we would doing anything else. We share with each other, help one another.

LATINO VALUES	ANGLO VALUES
Based on Catholicism, Spanish Colonialism, and respect for tradition	Based on Puritan, Protestant, and Calvinistic thinking of a new and free America
Interdependence	Independence
Family First	Me First
Family Helps Family	Helping Self Helps Family
Faith in God	Faith in Self and God
Humility	Self-Expression
Work Hard	Work Smart
Sacrifice	Pay Your Dues
Stability	What's New? What's Next?
Respect for Authority	Challenge Authority
Modesty	Toot Your Horn
God Loves the Poor	God Loves the Rich, Too
I Accept Life's Problems	I Solve Life's Problems
Small Success Is Good	Big Success Is Better
Whatever God Wants	What I Want, Too!
I Hope to Achieve	I Believe I Will Achieve
Vergüenza (a sense of shame)	What's That?
Sacrificio (sacrifice)	To a Point
Sufrimiento (suffering)	Avoid at All Costs
Sudor (sweat)	OK, But Not Forever
Responsabilidad (responsibility)	Of Course
Respeto (respect)	Earn It First
"Lo Que Dios Quiera" (Whatever God Wants)	"The Sky Is the Limit."

Source: Lionel Sosa

And we want to pass that on to our kids. We want them to share our feelings about the importance of culture, tradition, religion, and family.

When the legendary Hispanic adman Lionel Sosa headed up Ronald Reagan's Spanish-language political campaign, he learned something. Reagan recognized the importance of family values for Hispanics, and Sosa used that theme in the president's Spanish-language messages.

Since Reagan's campaign, Sosa has developed a chart comparing Latino and "Anglo-American" values, which we include here with his permission.

Sosa's chart highlights the fact that Latino values are rooted in our respect for tradition, faith in God, and love of family. And Mom is the center of the family.

Mamá's House

Forget macho. In Hispanic households, *Mamá* is the boss. If you want anybody in the house to buy something, you've got to sell her on it.

Hollywood did a great job of selling the idea of the dominant "macho man" lording over the house. Yeah, right. In fact, Hispanic men may fit the stereotype—they may be hot-blooded, hot-tempered, they may even be Latin lovers—but the person everybody listens to is Mom.

It's probably similar in other cultures that trace their origins to the Mediterranean. Publicly, the man rules. Privately, he may think he does. In reality, it's Mom. In the movie *My Big Fat Greek Wedding*, Toula's mother reveals the secret outsiders may not recognize: "The man is the head," she says. "But the woman is the neck, and she can turn the head any way she wants."

That's especially true in Hispanic households.

The Gatekeeper

In Latino families, Mom not only influences the father, she influences everyone.

That's why advertising aimed at anyone in the household needs to address Mom to be effective. Mom is the decision maker, even if it doesn't look like it. Mom may not flat-out say "no" or "get this," but her influence is absolute in most houses.

Obviously, Mother's Day is one of the biggest days of the year, even on the general market side. On the Hispanic side, the mom is the revered institution, to the point where she really is the gatekeeper, the *patrona*, the strong woman that makes things happen in the household.

That makes her a key point of entry.

You want the kids to buy? Target Mom.

It's the opposite of English-language marketing.

Take a look at the commercials during the cartoons. In

English, "Trix are for kids!" In Spanish, the folks at Honey Nut Cheerios fill their commercials for a kids' cereal with adults talking about the nutritional value and taste. The message is "your kids will like it and it's good for them," not "there's a prize in every box."

That's how it's done, whether the product is clothes, toys, or hamburgers.

This cultural nuance is critical. You can't just translate. In one English-language mayonnaise commercial, for example, a boy makes a sandwich for himself. "A Hispanic mother would never leave her young child alone with a knife," said Rosa Serrano, director of multicultural planning for Initiative Media in Los Angeles. In the Spanish version, the boy still makes the sandwich, but his mother keeps a watchful eye on him from across the kitchen.

The Trix Circus

Even the folks famous for their child-centric "Trix are for kids!" tagline recognized that the same approach wouldn't work with Hispanics.

The English pitch, with the unlucky cereal-loving rabbit, is a classic. To boost their sales to Latinos, however, Trix launched a nationwide campaign aimed at the whole family.

"Trix *circo mundial*," a full, traveling circus—with elephants, tigers, a big top, and everything—went town to town in heavily Hispanic markets, promoting the cereal. Trix's signature "silly rabbit" served as master of ceremonies. The one-ring, Latin-flavored circus included synchronized performing horses, trapeze acts, and acrobatics moving to salsa and merengue rhythms, in a bilingual format.

It was still a kids' cereal in Spanish, but the touring circus campaign recognized the need to tap into a core value among Latinos: family togetherness.

KIDS COUNT

That doesn't mean you can ignore the Hispanic emphasis on children. There are 9.5 million Latino families in the United States. Two-thirds have kids.

Unilever, the maker of Hellmann's, Lipton, and Skippy, among other brands, did a study of 799 Latino shoppers in Houston, Los Angeles, Miami, and New York.

"If she's not shopping with her children, she's thinking of them," the report concluded. "Consider rewarding her spending and pleasing her family with kid-item giveaways (sweet treats, crayons, picture books), or steep discounts on a kid-item with purchases of, say, $75 or more."

And remember, 20 percent of the nation's kids—one out of every five—are Hispanic. That's up from 17 percent in 2000, and 12 percent in 1990. In all, the number of Latinos under the age of 18 nearly doubled between 1990 and 2005, from 7.6 million to more than 14.4 million.

And there's no slowdown in sight. Hispanic kids are growing both in total number and in their proportion of all children in the U.S. The number of Hispanic kids is expected to hit almost 22 million by 2020. By 2050, demographers say Hispanics will account for 29 percent of the country's youth. Fully 81 percent of Latino households include children, compared to 67 percent of general population households.

That means a lot more moms shopping with kids, or at least thinking about them while she does.

WHO SAYS?

> Ask Hispanics what made them go for the Toyota over a Ford, or Cheer laundry detergent over Fab, and they're likely to tell you about a friend who had one, or about "Tia Carmen, whose wash always came out so clean."

We listen to the people we know.

The primary sources of influence for Latinos are people we have direct contact with—family, a friend, or someone we think of as an expert, like the local pharmacist, a mechanic, or a real estate agent. As we pointed out in the last chapter, it's true of politicians, and it's true of friends.

That's why network marketing works so well with Hispanics. Avon, Shaklee, and Tupperware sell well in the Latino market because each of them relies on contacts through friends and family. The sellers are people we know, or who come through people we know. That amounts to an implied endorsement, from someone we trust.

Health-care giant Johnson & Johnson used a variation on the theme when it launched its VidaNuestra campaign in 2005. It sent a 53-foot-long trailer made up to resemble a hacienda on a thirty-four-week cross-country tour. Inside, the trailer was designed to look like a six-room house belonging to the fictional Bueno family. Mom touts Splenda as a no-calorie alternative for sugar in their café; Grandpa Javier uses LifeScan's OneTouch for diabetes.

It's more than a demonstration of the many products and their uses. It's a subtle way of connecting on another level. The Buenos may be a fictional family, and they may not really be our friends, but having the endorsement of the entire clan gives it weight, nonetheless.

All Together Now

Hispanics stick together. We tend to be close-knit, and our idea of "family" includes not only the typical American nuclear family, but also a whole slew of near and distant relatives. And we like to get them all together regularly.

Sunday dinners, holidays, and special occasions don't just involve the kids, the grandparents, and mom and dad. Aunts, uncles, cousins, and in-laws all gather around. It's a time for food, fun, and bonding.

It's also a time for discussion. If Pedro is thinking of buying a new car, chances are, everyone will weigh in, right here.

When there's a big decision to be made, the entire family gets involved—it's the mom, the grandmother, the whole nine yards. Because of that, *la familia*, the family, is a very important vehicle to target, and market to, as opposed to individuals. And while it may mean more questions have to be answered, it also means you have more points of entry for your message.

In the 2006 Yankelovich MONITOR Multicultural Marketing Study, nearly half of all Hispanics said that "when it comes to important things in my life, I almost always seek the opinion of my extended family members," compared to 33 percent of non-Hispanic whites. Almost two-thirds (60 percent) of Hispanics (compared to 45 percent of African-Americans and 48 percent of non-Hispanic whites) said, "In my family, we discuss everyday things together before making a decision."

Procter & Gamble, one of the smartest and most effective at targeting Latinos, knows. It uses this to its advantage with a number of its products, from Gain detergent to Pampers.

The company's campaigns include a heavy dose of grassroots marketing, all aimed at spreading word of mouth. Young mothers get free samples at hospitals, and in-store demonstrations tout the benefits of P&G cleaners for busy housewives. They know, win one over and she becomes a powerful field rep for the company, sharing her experience and her opinion with the rest of the family.

MORE IN STORE

The importance of the family being together to make decisions comes into play even when it comes down to simple, day-to-day things, like a trip to the mall. In other words, Hispanics are the rat packs of consumers. We swarm into stores in groups to shop for all the things everybody wants and needs.

You know what that means to you. When you're selling to Hispanics, you have to think of the family, not just the individual consumer. You have to take into consideration the dynamics of a family situation.

By the same token, because more of us go along together when we go to the store we tend to buy more. That's true at Wal-Mart, Macy's, and the Food Maxx at Florin and Franklin in Sacramento, as store director Bart Brackin noticed.

"They don't just shop for TV dinners," Brackin told the *Sacramento Bee*. "It's a family thing, they bring the whole family, Mom and the kids and Dad and Grandma, and they fill up the shopping cart."

In its study of Hispanic shoppers, Unilever found that we shop with someone else—usually our kids—on 29 percent of all trips, compared to 23 percent in the general market.

And, the report continued, it's not just the shopping experience that involves family and food.

"From family to community, food for Hispanic Americans has an emotional and cultural significance that extends beyond eating. Hence, the Hispanic consumer thinks about every aspect of food shopping and preparation."

<u>In God We Trust</u>

Religion truly stands as a core value for Hispanics. We are churchgoers, overwhelmingly Christian, predominantly Catholic. But there also are a good number of Presbyterians and Baptists. Evangelical Christian denominations show increasing strength among Latinos. A study sponsored by the Pew Charitable Trust estimated that about 70 percent of Hispanics in the United States are Roman Catholic, and 22 percent are Protestant. Evangelical Christians account for the majority of those, 61 percent. Although much smaller in number, Jehovah's Witnesses and the Mormons have made considerable inroads among Hispanics. The study said more Hispanics are Mormon than United Methodist.

Regardless of the specific faith, Christianity plays a strong part in the Hispanic household, all across the country. Even though we come from different areas of different countries, religion is one of those elements that brings us together. It's a natural bond that we have, above language.

Holy Days are some of our biggest holidays, time for family gatherings (a blessing for retailers) and traditional meals and gift giving—at Christmas, Three Kings Day, even Easter. Families gather to celebrate holidays, birthdays, baptisms, first communions, graduations, and weddings.

And religion isn't just for special occasions. In a *Newsweek* poll, 42 percent of Latinos said they went to church once a week.

This has plenty of ramifications, both obvious and not so obvious.

At a gathering in San Francisco, Yankelovich Hispanic Monitoring told the nation's builders they should include churches as "part of the heart of the community when planning neighborhoods" in developments they want to sell to Latinos.

The Padre Show

Could you imagine having a top-rated talk show on a major broadcast network with a priest for a host? Not Dr. Phil. Not Oprah. Not Ellen. A priest. Dealing with the kind of topics you see on Jerry Springer—families struggling with drug addiction, infidelity, divorce.

That would never happen in general market television. But it did, in Spanish, on Telemundo. And it was a hit!

Padre Alberto has a last name, but like Oprah and Dr. Phil, no one really uses it. Padre Alberto is enough. (His last name, by the way, is Cutié—pronounced koo-tee-AY, not KYOO-tee, although in the world of television his youthful good looks certainly didn't hurt.)

The real, ordained Catholic priest at a Miami Beach church went nationwide with his show in 1998. Named, simply, *Padre Alberto*, the show tackled topics ranging from incest to the perils of plastic surgery.

Telemundo put it head-to-head against the Oprah of the Spanish-language universe, Cristina Saralegui.

It would be unimaginable on an English-language network. Never. No network exec who wanted to keep his job would say, "Let's put a religious advice show up against Oprah! Get Father McElroy from Holy Name!"

Even against such overwhelming competition, Padre Alberto's program lasted an incredible 400 shows, over three full years. That might not seem long in human years, but it's pretty darn good in television time. It's as long as *Star Trek* lasted before it was canceled, although it might seem like that one has gone on forever.

Padre Alberto's show was one of the best-rated shows for the sagging Telemundo network, which ran such a dismal second to Univision that on a good day it could only claim a 10 percent share of viewers. But after the struggling network switched hands for the second time in three years, the new owners wanted a change and canceled the show.

Still, the fact that it got on the air in the first place, and that it lasted as long as it did against the competition it faced, is a testament to the power of religion among Latinos.

R-E-S-P-E-C-T

Hispanic families also instill in their children the importance of honor and respect for authority and the elderly.

That's why the concept of nursing homes is really almost taboo among Hispanics. Your parents took care of you and you're going to take care of your parents. That's the way it is: The circle of Latino life.

The elders play an important part. And the concept of everyone signing off is critical and important.

This affects family decisions on a number of levels. Latinos don't send Grandma off to the nursing home, for the most part. And "the way things have always been done" imposes itself on everything from career decisions to brand loyalties.

It also gives products like Suavitel fabric softener and Kimberly-Clark's Huggies an edge among U.S. Hispanics. Both are dominant brands in Mexico. Immigrants bring their consumer habits with them and pass them on to their children.

P&G, the makers of competing Pampers and a host of other products, counters those ingrained patterns with concerted grass-roots and word-of-mouth efforts. It gives grandmothers in-store demonstrations of Bounty's "quicker picker upper" paper towels, aimed at overcoming their tendency to use dishrags or sponges for cleaning up spills.

SWEET 15

Our respect for our elders brings with it a respect for their ways. Latinos faithfully uphold the traditions of the past. It's a core characteristic. In a 2004 Pew survey, 93 percent of Hispanics said it was important to maintain their distinct cultures. In other words, to hold on to their traditions.

That plays out in a number of ways.

As we'll see in the next chapter, that love of tradition drives a key aspect of Hispanic families—the desire to keep Spanish alive in our homes.

Also, Latinos pretty much universally celebrate *quinces*, the Hispanic version of a debutante's ball. The elaborate dinners and parties can cost as much as a wedding, and parents spend years planning and preparing for them. It's big business for photographers, party planners, caterers, and dressmakers who create elegant gowns for the debutante's entourage. Sharp travel agents and cruise lines have targeted this tradition, creating packages that take hundreds of celebrants on sea voyages—and make hundreds of thousands of dollars for the ship owners.

Just goes to show you: good old-fashioned traditions can be good new-fashioned moneymakers.

ADDING IT UP

Whether you're thinking about your employees or your customers, the key is: we have strong family values.

Work-life issues take on a different significance with Hispanics. Commitments to family matter to everyone, of course, but the emphasis on the family connection may make it difficult for a Latino worker to accept a job transfer that will take him or her away from the clan.

Family comes first. And Mom takes center stage in the Hispanic family world. To sell to Latinos, target her. Remember the difference between the English-language cereal ads and the Spanish-language ones. It takes more than translation. You have to keep the key in mind. Mom cares about her kids' nutrition, not the secret decoder ring in the bottom of the box.

Whether you're selling toys, kids' clothes, or laptops, show her the product benefits that are important to her. That the kids are happy, comfortable, and look cool in your clothing is important—she wants them to be happy. But if the clothes are stain resistant, that's even better. Your toys are fun? Great. Show Mom enjoying some much-needed leisure time while her kids are safe and happy playing with them.

Kids are her priority. As Unilever found, even if she's not with them, she's thinking about them. That means she's going to be attuned and receptive to ads and information about them, and products and services for them. In other words, Latino moms are ripe targets for anything having to do with her kids, all the time. Don't think your toy commercial needs to run only during cartoons and kid shows. They can be equally effective during a *telenovela*.

Another thing to remember when you're dealing with Hispanics is the power of word of mouth. We value the opinions of the people we trust. You can use that to your advantage. Think about ways to tap into that network and create favorable "buzz" about your product or service. A pharmacy, clinic, or dentist's office can easily offer health fairs that help cement its reputation as a friendly neighborhood expert.

What about you? Can your company provide tastings at stores or festivals to prompt word of mouth? What about product giveaways? Procter & Gamble and Kimberly-Clark make sure that new mothers get samples of their competing disposable diapers. So do the makers of Similac and Enfamil baby formula. Detergent and shampoo makers regularly mail out test packets of their product. They know. A favorable impression nets a new customer. With Latinos, that impression can attract several more as the word spreads.

Levi's Dockers put this key to work in the fall of 2005. The company sent pants, shirt, socks, and a belt to 1,000 selected Hispanics across the country. In return, the recipients had to wear the pants, talk to their friends and family about them, and tell Levi's how it went. They wanted to generate "buzz."

Could it have backfired? No. If they liked it, they'd spread the good news. If they didn't, Levi's got immediate feedback. Any way you look at it, it was a win: Either they generated powerful word-of-mouth advertising, they gathered valuable market research, or both.

Remember, too, the importance of family influencers. It's common for just about everyone to weigh in on decisions. They can be formal family powwows to discuss a move or vacation plans. Or they can be informal one-on-one chats about the pros and cons of a car someone wants to buy. We get input from the clan.

Your marketing campaign should take that into account. When you target Hispanics, your ads can gain positive traction if they show the whole family benefiting from and enjoying your product or service. What they think matters. The Office of National Drug Control Policy used this concept with a TV, print, and radio campaign aimed at kids. The idea: If you do drugs, you let your family down.

Our respect for our elders is a double-edged sword for you. Their influence can work for you if they have a positive opinion of you. The opposite, of course, is also true.

Ingrained beliefs or consumer habits can be just as harmful. A grandmother who used Palmolive dishwashing detergent will push her daughters and daughters-in-law to do the same. To get them to switch to your brand, you'll have to persuade the elder. Give her the sample. Consider an advertising campaign that shows a grandmother discovering that your product is better and showing how much she cares for her daughter by convincing her to use it. The message: She cares enough to drop the old ways so her daughter can have a better life.

We also tend to shop together—at the auto dealer, at the department store, at the grocery store, and the mall. That brings several considerations, and several opportunities.

Your target consumers may be English-dominant, but they're likely to be shopping with influencers, like Mom or Grandma, who only speak Spanish. Spanish-language signage targeting the companion will help sell to your intended customer.

Also, since we travel in groups, that automatically means we're bringing more potential customers into your outlet. You can double up your sales by offering "buy one, get the second half off" deals to hit both the target and influencer.

The importance of religion in our lives opens up several possibilities for you. Religious holidays and family celebrations provide chances to sell cakes, piñatas, and decorations, along with cards and gifts. And I'm not talking about just Christmas, Easter, and birthdays. Don't forget Three Kings Day, on Jan. 6. Many Hispanic families give children a small gift that day, supposedly left by the three wise men. Advertising that emphasizes that tradition leading up to the holiday can help you move toys, candy, and kids' clothes, among other things.

Also, feast days for patron saints, like Mexico's Virgin of Guadalupe (Dec. 12), include celebrations and family gatherings—with plenty of food and libations. Hallmark recognized how many Latinos name their children after saints, and honor that namesake's feast day. It seized the chance to make more sales by offering Spanish-language cards commemorating *El día de tu santo*, Your Saint's Day.

One of the most important religious celebrations of the year for Mexicans is *El día de los muertos*, or the Day of the Dead. Although many here confuse it with Halloween, it's not. It's more like an elaborate Memorial Day, a time for remembering and honoring the deceased, which actually spreads over two days, Nov. 1 and 2. And just as retailers have caught on to the opportunities that come from Memorial Day picnics and family gatherings, the Day of the Dead is a tradition with plenty of sales potential. It calls for colorful decorations and lively family reunions that include displays of skeletons, wreaths, crosses, candles, and flowers, along with a variety of sweets, baked goods, and a feast.

The significance of religion also offers a way to connect with Latinos in your community. You can sponsor church picnics, put up prizes for raffles, put up a booth and give away samples at festivals.

The safe bet for any business is to remember that our family values affect our every decision. Taking them into account is good for your bank account.

Chapter 6

WE WANT TO BE COURTED IN THE LANGUAGE WE MAKE LOVE IN

Advertisers always look for the hot button. They want to find the trigger point that will make an individual react, to buy the goods or services that are being offered. For Latinos, the first and foremost is language. We want to be courted in the language we make love in.

For some, that's English. For most of us, it's *español*.

This is probably the hottest topic among marketers today: Should I use English or Spanish to reach out?

The answer is both. There's a place for English in your Hispanic marketing plan, no doubt. But you'll hit many more Latinos, across the broadest spectrum of young to old, in Spanish. Spanish remains the lingua franca of U.S. Hispanics, no matter where they were born. Four out of five Latinos in this country speak some Spanish. Of those, two out of three prefer it.

That's out of *all* the Hispanics in the United States—

immigrants, their children, and their children's children. Of the 38 million or so Latinos over age 5 in the United States, almost 33 million are bilingual or speak Spanish only.

I know it's hard to believe. But those are census bureau numbers, backed up by studies by the Pew Hispanic Center, Yankelovich, Inc., the Roslow Research Group, Synovate, and Geoscape International, to name a few. Those are some pretty well respected researchers. And they all came up with similar results.

Sure, the percentage of Spanish speakers declines significantly by the time you get to the third generation and beyond. But third-generation Hispanics who don't speak any Spanish at all are less than 12 percent of the total market. They may be low-hanging fruit, but there's a heck of a lot of tree you're missing if you stick to English only.

That's a bad idea. Ask the networks.

SEEING IS BELIEVING

While ratings for the English-language networks continue to erode, Spanish-language networks are gaining viewers. Univision reported that its prime-time 18–49 audience grew 17 percent in 2005, much more than ABC, NBC, CBS, or Fox.

Univision consistently ranks fifth and often fourth of all broadcast networks in the 18–49 age bracket in prime time. It regularly beats WB and UPN. In 2005, it beat them all on fifty-five nights, placing first among 18- to 34-year-olds.

That's a demo where the Spanish-language networks are particularly strong and growing. Univision counts 1.4 million of them as regular viewers in prime time. Its prime-time *telenovela*, *Barrera de Amor*, premiered with 18- to 34-year-old ratings that were second only to *American Idol*.

That's good for the Spanish-language nets, today and tomorrow. Univision knows that today's 18- to 34-year-olds are tomorrow's 34- to 49-year-olds. And tomorrow's 18- to 34-year-olds are more likely to be Hispanic as well. Hispanics are the fastest-growing segment of the population, and more than a third are under 18. And, study after study has shown, they're more likely to hold on to their Spanish-language roots.

They're doing it on their own, and their parents are pushing them to. More than half of the third-generation Latinos, ones whose parents are also U.S.-born, say they want their kids to learn Spanish—even if they don't speak it themselves. In fact, in a Yankelovich study in 2005, 65 percent of Hispanics said they feel "my native language is an important aspect of my culture and traditions that is important to preserve." Seven out of ten said the Spanish language is more important to them than it was five years ago.

Caliente Is Hot

Hispanics, like most consumers, make their decisions based on emotions. We may discuss all the logical reasons for buying a sedan or a minivan, but in the end we pick the one we connect with emotionally, the one we "like" the most.

Spanish is our language of emotion. It's home. Mom. Love. And passion. Make that Passion, with a capital P. English may connect to our brains, but Spanish connects to our hearts. Connect to our hearts and you connect to our pockets. Take it to the bank.

Even if we only speak English, Spanish connects with us on a visceral level. It reaches our roots and brings out a smile. It has the same effect on us that Italian has on Italian-Americans, even fifth-generation ones. Their Italian may be limited to "pass the Parmesan," but they still perk up an ear when they hear, "*Mama mia!*" They feel the words "that's *amore*" in their souls. "*Paisan*" rings a potent hereditary bell. It's a hot button that tells them, "We're one of you. We know what you like." It sets off a series of favorable reminders: of home, family, culture.

They don't know very many words, though. So the words that work are more limited than they are with a fluent Italian speaker. They share a limited dictionary.

The same holds true with Latinos. Spanish connects with our souls—even with those of us who don't speak very much. We all use the same dictionary, even if it's a smaller one.

Beck's beer made the point perfectly with a recent ad. It just showed a bottle and the words: *Vives en inglés. Pero sientes en español.* You live in English. But you feel in Spanish.

Underneath, the tagline added: *Así eres.* That's the way you are.

Great lines. And true. Beck's knows. Spanish connects with Hispanics of every generation.

It also affects our perception of you and your company. Remember the reaction when then-candidate George W. Bush spoke Spanish? It endeared him to us. When we hear you speaking in Spanish, it tells us you noticed us. It tells us you care enough to try. It says you know what's important to us, and that it's important to you. That's important.

Español, Alive and Well

Some say, why bother? They expect Spanish to give way to English as Latinos become increasingly assimilated. They've been waiting a long time.

Twenty-five years ago, in the early days of Spanish-language media in this country, everyone talked about Spanish having a ten-year lifespan. We were all going to be out of it, and working for NBC. Here we are twenty-five years later, and people are still talking about it having a ten-year lifespan. And by the way, many in the Hispanic media business are working for NBC, which now owns Telemundo, the country's second Spanish-language television network.

The reality is that Spanish shows no signs of dying out. In fact, just the opposite. In hard numbers, according to the census, the number of people aged 5 and up who speak a language other than English at home actually increased by 47 percent between 1990 and 2000. Most of them, 59.9 percent, speak Spanish.

And it's going to continue increasing, every day.

An exclusive study conducted by the Roslow Research Group shows that the number of Spanish-dominant and bilingual Latinos will go up by 45 percent over the next two decades. By 2025, more than 40 million Spanish speakers will live in the United States. That's another 12.5 million Spanish speakers since 2000—more than the population of Pennsylvania.

It's not just because of continuing immigration. Unlike other immigrant groups, even third-generation Hispanics continue to speak Spanish in extraordinarily large numbers.

The study based its forecast on a statistical analysis of existing information from the Pew Hispanic Center's 2004 estimates, the census, and a variety of other sources, along with reasonable assumptions about such factors as future immigration estimates, life expectancy and fertility rates, population aging, and lastly, Spanish-language use by generation/place of birth.

Among the results:

□ Fully two-thirds of Hispanics 5 and older will speak Spanish as a first language or as comfortably as they do English twenty years from now.
□ On average, 35 percent of third-generation Latinos in the United States speak Spanish.

- The 18-and-older Spanish-speaking population will increase by 53 percent, to 15.2 million by 2025.
- The key 18- to 49-year-old demographic will grow by 7.5 million to include 59 percent of all the Spanish speakers.
- Another 1.5 million will be in the youngest demographic group, the 5- to 17-year-olds.

WE WANT OUR MTV

MTV sees the potential.

The premier youth-oriented network, which practically defined television targeted at 12- to 34-year-olds, launched the bilingual MTV Tr3s network in the fall of 2006. That's right, bilingual. Pronounced *tres*, meaning "three" in Spanish, the reformatted and redesigned version of its Spanish-language MTV en Español airs English *and* Spanish music videos, lifestyle series, and documentaries.

At first glance, the move from strictly Spanish to a bilingual—and bicultural—format seems to be a rejection of Spanish. Actually, it's just the opposite. It's a testament to the vibrancy and vitality of Spanish among the next generation of Latinos in this country.

Why? Because if it were strictly about language, about delivering and receiving information in English, they already did that with the original MTV. Why would anyone go to the enormous expense of putting out a whole new network, with the colossal cost of equipment, technicians, talent, and everything else that it takes, if they've already got one that satisfies that market?

The programming change recognized the bicultural character and taste of a young Latin audience that enjoys English-language rock and hip hop, but clings to its Spanish-language roots.

The format itself is nothing new. LATV and Telemundo's sister network, Mun2, have offered variations for years. Even MTV en Español added a mix of English-language music videos to its mainstream Spanish-language lineup in 2005. But the very fact that the 800-pound gorilla that virtually invented programming for a youth audience would adopt a similar programming format is an indication of the reality and significance of Hispanics in this country.

It's about Hispanic U.S.A., a whole new cultural landscape evolving in this country, with roots in both the American and Latino traditions. This new demographic phenomenon is as distinctly American as American culture itself, yet distinctly Latin as well—and determined to hold on to the Spanish language.

To put it simply, as the head of MTV Tr3s did when the programming change was announced, "Hispanic youth is very comfortable with both languages."

Mun2, Telemundo's cable offshoot, calls them YLAs— Young Latin Americans. In a yearlong, three-part study, it concluded that YLAs live in a hybrid world—American and Latin, speaking English and Spanish. They know Dance Dance Revolution, but they also know Don Omar, their mom's *tele-*

novela, and 400 of the 1,000 songs on their iPods are by Latin artists. They identify with Latino family values, like hard work and respecting family, and more than two-thirds want a stronger connection to their culture.

"We are at the tipping point of an emerging new lifestyle category that will greatly affect American and global culture. Young Latino Americans are in the process of innovating their own customized culture that encompasses music, language, fashion, food, entertainment, and beyond," said Sharon Lee, Co-President/Co-Founder of Look-Look which conducted the study. "It's an exciting time and this young community is absolutely aware that they are the next big thing."

Now, MTV Tr3s is coming after them full bore, billing itself as the "fusion of American and Latin music and cultures." It's aiming for 5.5 million homes half the Hispanic households in the United States—through a hybrid cable-satellite-broadcast distribution model that takes advantage of parent company Viacom's ten newly purchased Texas and California stations. That's a leap from MTV Español's 3.1 million Hispanic households.

"MTV Tr3s will be the validation, *voz* and *vida* of young U.S. Latinos by celebrating their influence, cultures, and languages," Lucia Ballas-Traynor, the network's general manager, said in announcing the new venture.

What she means is that the battle for this massive market segment is on, and English is not enough. To win here, *se habla español*.

THE 50–25–25 RULE

Here's an easy way to think of how the market breaks down:

Half speak Spanish. Another quarter are bilingual and bi-cultural. The rest speak English.

I call it the 50–25–25 Rule. I came up with it after I noticed that every study, every survey, shows similar results, give or take a few points: 50 percent of U.S. Hispanics are Spanish-dominant. Another 25 percent speak English and Spanish equally. The remaining 25 percent are English-dominant.

Some studies count it a little higher. Some a little lower. Synovate counts 56 percent who speak only Spanish at home, 26 percent who speak both, and 18 percent only English. Geoscape International comes up with a similar breakdown—about 83 percent who speak Spanish or both. The census doesn't break out the Spanish-onlys, but it counts about 74 percent who speak Spanish or Spanish and English at home.

Even more stunning, the census reported that more than one-quarter of the population in seven states spoke a language other than English at home. Eight states had over 1 million non-English speakers, including California, which had 12.4 million. And the number of non-English speakers at least doubled in six states between 1990 and 2000. Sixty percent of them are speaking Spanish.

PILGRIMS

One reason for the continuing increase in Spanish speakers is the continuing arrival of new Spanish-speaking immigrants. In 2003, about 33 million foreign-born people lived in the United States, accounting for nearly 12 percent of the population, census statistics show. Fifty-three percent of those immigrants were born in Latin America. Half had arrived since 1990.

And there are no signs of it slowing.

Indeed, the Hispanic U.S.A. study pointed out, "recent analysis has shown that between 2000 and 2005, the annual increase in the number of Hispanic immigrants has actually outpaced increases from the 1990s."

Traditionally, the census and other demographers have underestimated the rate of immigration. Just before the national count in 2000, the Census Bureau predicted that the number of new arrivals coming each year would peak in 1999. Based on that, the bureau estimated there would be just over 38 million Latinos in the country in 2005.

Wrong.

They missed by almost 5 million. That's like missing Chicago and Houston—together. Or all of Colorado. And that's a pretty good-sized market, all by itself.

Talking Tradition

There's another reason Spanish keeps going strong. It's that tradition thing we talked about in the last chapter. Latinos tend to keep Spanish alive in their households.

Children of Spanish-dominants tend to be bilingual. In fact, according to Spanish broadcast giant Univision, 75 percent of 18- to 48-year-old Hispanic adults speak Spanish at home. Their children do, too. Naturally, going to school here, those kids tend to speak English as well. But they also speak Spanish. A HispanTelligence study found that the number of bilinguals has grown six percentage points since 1995, to 63 percent, and is likely to jump to 67 percent by 2010.

Geoscape International found similar results. In its 2006 geo-demographic database, an analysis of demographic data down to the block group, it found that:

- The vast majority of Hispanics are bilingual or Spanish-dependent—82 percent nationwide.
- More than two-thirds of those prefer to speak Spanish— 69.6 percent.

At least part of the reason lies with the kids. Generally, demographers and sociologists use a three-generation rule. They count immigrants as first-generation, their kids as second, and their kids' kids as third. And, the way they figure it, once both parents are U.S.-born, the likelihood that their kids will speak a foreign language as well or better than English virtually disappears. Historically, that's a pretty good rule. Until now.

Latinos break the mold.

Roslow has done extensive research in this area. It has found—repeatedly—that about 79 percent of second-generation Hispanics are bilingual or Spanish-dominant. Even more surprisingly, so are more than a third (35 percent) of third-generation Latinos.

That's huge.

Hispanic Heartland

The result of those two factors, births and immigration, is having an impact far beyond the old "Hispanic Smile" markets like L.A., New York, Miami, and Texas.

It's happening in such far-flung communities as Fayetteville, Ark., where the non-English-speaking population shot up a phenomenal 386 percent during the '90s. It's happening in Utah, Tennessee, Colorado, Oregon, Idaho, Virginia, and Nebraska.

The Hispanic U.S.A. study detailed the expected growth of Spanish speakers in the top twenty-five Hispanic markets in the country. The projections show striking, across-the-board increases—40 to 55 percent growth in every one. Los Angeles, the biggest, leads the way in terms of sheer numbers. But such

SPANISH-SPEAKING HISPANICS POPULATION ESTIMATES BY MARKET

Persons 5 Years of Age & Over (in thousands)

Market	2005	2015	2025	% Shift 2005–2025
Los Angeles	5,137	6,348	7,306	+42%
New York	2,883	3,569	4,140	+44%
Miami-Fort Lauderdale	1,267	1,574	1,819	+44%
Houston	1,179	1,485	1,761	+49%
Chicago	1,188	1,480	1,685	+42%
Dallas-Fort Worth	1,021	1,280	1,519	+49%
San Francisco-Oakland-San Jose	960	1,195	1,381	+44%
Phoenix (Prescott)	794	1,001	1,211	+53%
San Antonio	790	977	1,107	+40%
Harlingen-Weslaco-Brownsville-McAllen	668	839	1,016	+52%
San Diego	610	773	939	+54%
Sacramento-Stockton-Modesto	608	759	909	+50%
Fresno-Visalia	604	755	856	+42%
El Paso (Las Cruces)	488	620	733	+50%
Denver	478	592	691	+45%
Albuquerque-Santa Fe	454	560	640	+42%
Washington D.C. (Hagerstown)	394	498	603	+53%
Philadelphia	359	451	543	+51%
Orlando-Daytona Beach-Melbourne	321	410	498	+55%
Atlanta	328	412	496	+51%
Tampa-St. Pete (Sarasota)	311	397	463	+49%
Austin	294	374	456	+55%
Las Vegas	288	366	445	+55%
Boston (Manchester)	271	342	420	+55%
Tucson (Sierra Vista)	255	320	367	+44%

Source: Roslow Research Group.

major cities as Boston, Las Vegas, and Austin top the charts with an expected 55 percent growth in each. San Diego, Phoenix, Washington, D.C., and Atlanta are close behind.

Prime Time

While population increases and tradition drive the continued growth of Spanish, Spanish-language media helps maintain it.

Spanish speakers can get all the news, information, and entertainment they want in Spanish. Spanish-language newscasts are now number one in L.A., New York, and Miami. *El Piolin* has the most popular morning radio show in L.A., by far. Spanish-language newspapers are springing up in corners of the Carolinas. Clear Channel is switching Oldies and Pop stations in Orlando and Atlanta to Spanish music formats.

And Spanish-language media is a self-perpetuating machine: The more Spanish speakers there are, the more the media grow. As they grow, they attract more viewers, listeners, and readers. The fact is that Spanish-language media content is very relevant to Latinos all across the country.

A nationwide survey of Hispanics by the research firm Bendixen & Associates found that 87 percent of adult Latinos access Spanish-language television, radio, or newspapers on a regular basis.

Even that is growing. The study found that Spanish-language radio and newspapers are rapidly increasing their penetration. More than a quarter (29 percent) of Hispanic adults said they now prefer Spanish-language newspapers to their English-language counterparts.

Univision's audience has soared by 44 percent since 2001, by 146 percent in the 18- to 34-year-old group. Many of those viewers have come from English-language networks, whose audiences have declined.

Among Hispanics, top-rated English-language shows may not even register. As the networks headed into their blockbuster season finales in 2005, International Communications Research polled 832 Latinos nationwide. Only four English-language shows made it into the top forty among Latino viewers. *American Idol* led the pack at number twenty-nine, with *Desperate Housewives*, *CSI*, and *The Simpsons* trailing behind.

This past summer, Univision did it again. In the last week of July, the *telenovela Fea Mas Bella* beat CBS's *The Unit*, NBC's *Medium*, and ABC's *Making a Music Star*. And, show-for-show that week, everything else on Univision beat everything it was up against on those three networks, and the WB and UPN. The whole week. Only Fox had more 18- to 34-year-old prime-time viewers.

Of course, the WB and UPN are no surprise. Ever since Nielsen Media Research started counting the English- and Spanish-language networks together in one group instead of separately, Univision has consistently gotten better ratings than either of those two.

On average that week, Univision had 3 million viewers in prime time, Telemundo had 1 million, and TeleFutura had half a million.

That's a lot of eyeballs.

BILL GATES *HABLA ESPAÑOL*

Bill Gates is a pretty smart guy. He's the co-founder of Microsoft, the richest man on the planet. So, if he thought that putting up as much as $12 billion to buy the Spanish-language television network Univision would be a worthwhile investment, it must mean something.

It does: Bill Gates understands Spanish. Don't get me wrong, he may not speak Spanish, but he knows what it means—at least what it means in the United States, in media, and in keeping up with the fastest growing market in the country.

In case you didn't follow the goings-on, Univision put itself on the auction block last February. In May, Mexican media giant Grupo Televisa, which already owned 11 percent of Univision and provides the bulk of its programming, revealed that it had joined with four investors to make a bid. One of those four was Gates's private investment group, Cascade Investment.

Gates owns a small chunk of Televisa—about 6.35 million shares, worth just a few dollars under $511 million. And, through the Bill and Melinda Gates Foundation, he already owned a $2.9 million sliver of Univision stock.

But the fact that he was willing to join in on a takeover of Univision means even more. Of course, Gates wasn't the first to see its potential. Viacom, headed by another pretty savvy media czar, Sumner Redstone, made a play for Univision (rumored at $7 billion) back in 2002 and got turned down.

In the end, Gates and group lost out. Univision went for $13.7 billion to four private equity firms, a consortium that included billionaire investor Haim Saban, the Power Rangers guy. The price had some squawking, but it may not be unreasonable.

Back when NBC bought Univision's rival Telemundo for $2.7 billion in 2001, it seemed like a lot for a network running a distant second in the ratings race. At the time, Univision boasted about 80 percent of the Hispanic viewers tuning in to prime time, and Wall Street valued the network at about $6.4 billion, including debt.

Back then, Hispanic buying power stood at about $500 billion. Today we're closing in on double that. Hispanics, and our buying power, has surpassed every other minority group. And while Univision's share of the ratings has dipped to about 71 percent, we've added some 6 million pairs of eyeballs to the market. Despite its overall decline in share, Univision's viewership has grown 67 percent in the last decade.

Bill Gates knows the importance of Univision and Spanish. And he's not alone. While advertisers were rethinking their spending on English-language networks at the 2006 upfront marketplace in New York, wondering if their money might be better spent on the Internet, the Spanish-language nets nabbed a 50 percent increase in sales, to $1.8 billion.

New advertisers, like PeoplePC and AstraZeneca's Nexium, dove in. Major players, like Procter & Gamble and Johnson & Johnson, added brands to the Hispanic TV mix. The makers of Budweiser and Miller both doubled their Spanish-language TV spending over the year before, to $17.5 million and $36.4 million, respectively. Coors nearly tripled its budget to $11.2 million. In all, Hispanic TV and print advertising grew twice as fast as English-language media in 2005.

So when Bill Gates hears Spanish, he knows what it means. It's where the smart money is placing its bets.

Talk to Me

There are now close to seventy Spanish-language cable stations and dozens of local independent stations with Spanish-language programming. Everything from ESPN Deportes to the History Channel en Español. Nineteen of them started in 2004 alone. They're targeting soccer fans with GolTV, kids with Sorpresa!, and offering inspirational programming with TBN Enlace and La Familia.

The point? Spanish-language television is following the same pattern English-language has. It's proliferating, and increasingly, targeting specific niches within the larger Latino market.

For example, the Discovery Channel launched a spin-off cable network in Spanish in 1998. Seven years later, it added two more, aimed at what it identified as "underserved, underprogrammed" sectors: women and children.

It molded *"Viajar y Vivir"* (Travel and Living) as a lifestyle channel for women, with travel, food, and home decoration programs.

"Discovery Kids *en español*" was designed to capture children with educational and family-friendly educational programs. It starts the day with shows aimed at preschoolers, goes after older kids after school, then switches to family-oriented animal and nature programs in the evening.

The list of programming fare is long, varied, and growing.

That's good news for you, if you want to target your advertising at a specific market segment. Instead of firing scattershot across the whole spectrum in hopes of flying past desirable eyeballs, you can aim more precisely.

Singing Along

Radio isn't far behind.

Atlanta's newest radio station, Viva 105.7, launched in September '04, serving up a mix of music by Spanish pop artists, along with a smattering by Mexican regional bands. Talk about 0 to 60: Its Arbitron share went from 1.6 to 11.3 immediately as it shot to number two among 18- to 34-year-olds in the metropolitan area—not just Spanish-speaking 18- to 34-year-olds, all of them.

The station's owner noticed. Clear Channel Communications announced plans to convert at least two dozen of its general-market radio stations to Latino formats in 2005, more than doubling its number of Hispanic stations.

And, as radio moved onto satellite, so did Spanish. Both Sirius and XM offer various channels programmed in Spanish.

Turn on your radio. See what you find. Across the country, the number of Spanish-language radio stations more than doubled since 1998, from 302 then to well over 700 today.

That's because Hispanic radio shines in the otherwise lackluster radio world. Revenue in Spanish-language radio grew more than four times as fast as the general market in the last few years.

The fact is that Spanish-language radio is one of the fastest growing mediums in America today, with Spanish language radio stations dominating the ratings game all across the country.

Print Power

People en Español, the Spanish-language magazine with the highest circulation in the country, started almost by accident, thanks to an English-language experiment.

When the Latin pop star Selena died in 1995, *People* magazine put out a special commemorative issue. It sold a million

TOP 10 HISPANIC MAGAZINES BY CIRCULATION

Rank	Magazine	Avg. 2005 Paid Circulation	% Chg
1	*People en Español*	469,110	3.3
2	*Latina*	416,162	17.7
3	*Reader's Digest Selecciones*	354,699	−2.1
4	*TV y Novelas Estados Unidos*	175,765	25.4
5	*Vanidades*	155,917	5.5
6	*Cosmopolitan en Español*	139,844	11.9
7	*¡Mira!*	116,866	−1.7
8	*Hispanic Business*	63,649	−1.0
9	*TV Notas*	56,666	2.1
10	*Buenhogar*	49,325	NA

Table includes Audit Bureau of Circulations monitored magazines only, for six months ended Dec. 31, 2005, versus six months ended Dec. 31, 2004.

Source: *Advertising Age.* "Hispanic Fact Pack. Annual Guide to Hispanic Marketing & Media, 2006 Edition." July 17, 2006.

copies. In English. But *People*'s parent, Time Inc., saw an opportunity, in Spanish. It saw the Selena sales (the special, seventy-six-page Selena edition outsold a similar tribute for Audrey Hepburn) as a clue to the growing importance of Hispanic culture in the U.S.

It launched *People en Español* soon after to test the waters. The hunch paid off. Five years later, circulation topped 400,000 per month, reaching an estimated 4 million Latino readers.

Now there's *Shape*, *Cosmopolitan*, and *Vogue en español*. Even *Reader's Digest* launched a stand-alone Spanish-language edition just for the U.S. market, even though it already had editions in Mexico and Spain.

Doing It Daily

Newspapers followed a different route, but are finding similar success.

Circulation of Spanish-language dailies has more than tripled since 1990. Ad revenues have grown more than sevenfold over the past decade. Analysts predict that trend will continue well into the future.

Just look at the growth of *La Opinion* in Los Angeles, *El Nuevo Herald* in Miami, and *La Prensa* in New York. Not to mention hundreds of dailies and weeklies that have popped up all around the country.

The big media companies don't need to speak Spanish to understand potential profits. The *Chicago Tribune* publishes *Hoy* in New York, Chicago, and Los Angeles, as well as *El Sentinel* in Fort Lauderdale and Orlando. The *Washington Post* bought *El Tiempo Latino* in 2004.

El Internet

The move online started a bit slowly among Hispanics. But by 2006, the trend was obvious: Latinos had discovered media's new frontier and were making inroads.

The third annual AOL/Roper Hispanic Cyberstudy, released that summer, found that Internet use by Latinos was quickly catching up with the general market. And the ones who made the connection may like it even more than non-Hispanics. The survey of 603 respondents found that Latinos were more likely to have broadband connections and spent more time online at home—9.2 hours a week, compared to 8.5 hours for the general online population.

Two-thirds said it's important to have Spanish online content. And, significantly, even English-speaking Hispanics said they took special notice of online ads in Spanish. Nearly a third of the bilingual Latinos in the survey said they "pay more attention to ads when they're in Spanish than when they're only in English."

In this area, too, Univision dominates. Nielsen Media Research ranked it as the most trafficked Spanish-language website among bilingual and Spanish-dominant Hispanics 16 and older. And last summer, it announced a multi-year agreement to incorporate Google's search products on its site, promising to broaden its reach.

TOP 10 ADVERTISERS ON HISPANIC WEBSITES			
By measured U.S. Web ad spending			
Rank	Company	2005 Ad Spending	% Chg
1	General Motors Corp.	$4,925.9	347.2
2	France Telecom	2,469.1	0.8
3	Ford Motor Co.	2,050.2	43.7
4	IAC/InterActiveCorp	1,847.7	−23.4
5	Allstate Corp.	1,740.5	NA
6	Englishtown School	1,693.5	55.4
7	AFP	1,654.4	NA
8	Toyota Motor Corp.	1,537.5	−11.7
9	Verizon Communications	1,535.0	131.5
10	Mosaico	1,521.6	−2.8

Dollars are in thousands. Measured Web ad spending from TNS Media Intelligence. Percent change is computed from 2004 data. TNS monitors 17 Hispanic sites.

Source: Advertising Age. "Hispanic Fact Pack. Annual Guide to Hispanic Marketing & Media, 2006 Edition." July 17, 2006.

But the Telemundo Yahoo! portal brought together the strengths of both partners, bringing the network's existing TV content to the web and combining it with Yahoo!'s search tools and mail and messenger services. In an indication of things to come, the site also included original made-for-broadband video content. T-Max, one of the first examples, posted fifteen-minute shows about celebrity events.

Take Me to the Concert

Just ask Kate Ramos who heads up the Hispanic division for Live Nation, which just happens to be the world's largest producer of concerts, and she will tell you that her division is one of the fastest growing in the company. Artists like Shakira, Marc Anthony, Enrique Iglesias, Ricardo Arjona, Juanes, and Paulina Rubio are selling out full-blown arenas across the country. You may recognize only a couple of the names listed, but to the majority of Hispanics these are all household names.

There are synergies at work here as well. In 2006, a Univision *novela* titled *Rebelde* (Rebel) had a story line that included a fictional musical group RBD. It was not long before life was imitating art, and the fictional group came to life with record sales and concert tours that are breaking all sorts of records. And it all happened in Spanish, right here in our backyard.

Cutting the Clutter

The meaning is clear. Spanish is here to stay. And growing.

And that's good news for you, if you want your business to grow.

Even with the proliferation of media targeting Latinos,

TOP 10 WEB PROPERTIES AMONG SPANISH-LANGUAGE PREFERRED USERS

By number of unique visitors

Rank	Property	Unique Visitors in Thousands	% Reach
1	Yahoo! sites	2,873	84.4
2	MSN-Microsoft sites	2,762	81.2
3	Google sites	2,225	65.4
4	Time Warner Network	2,136	62.8
5	eBay	1,656	48.7
6	Univision.com	1,553	45.7
7	Terra Networks	1,216	35.7
8	Ask Network	1,043	30.7
9	Wanadoo sites	956	28.1
10	Amazon sites	908	26.7

Data from comScore Media Metrix. Unique visitors are in thousands. Percent reach is the percent of all Hispanic Internet users who prefer Spanish (3.4 million) or English (8.2 million) who visited the property for the month of May 2006.

Source: Advertising Age. "Hispanic Fact Pack. Annual Guide to Hispanic Marketing & Media, 2006 Edition." July 17, 2006.

the Spanish-language landscape remains relatively uncluttered. Your message gets heard.

If you look at the vehicles that are bombarding a non-Hispanic on any given day, it's in the dozens and dozens and dozens: through cable, through over-the-air television, through radio, through the Internet, and through outdoor advertising. It goes on and on and on.

Spanish speakers get hit with much, much less. So, in Spanish, your message is not caught up in as much clutter as it is in English.

Think of it this way: If you're the only one talking in a stadium, everyone hears you. If everybody's shouting, your voice gets lost in the crowd. In English, lots of people are shouting.

Español = Effective

Ads in Spanish work. They're incredibly effective—with adults, teens, Spanish-dominants, and bilinguals alike. Even English-dominants respond better to Spanish ads.

Several studies by the Roslow Research Group confirm it. Commercials in Spanish are 55 percent more effective at increasing ad awareness levels than commercials in English. They're 50 percent more effective in message communication. And ads received in Spanish are four and a half times more persuasive than ones received in English.

And not just among adults. Roslow specifically examined how teens reacted. The results: Commercials in Spanish are 40 percent more effective at increasing ad awareness levels and twice as persuasive as ones in English.

In a novel, attention-grabbing marketing move in early 2005, the auto website Vehix.com went after young male

Latinos on cable's Spike TV during showings of *WWE Raw* and *WWE Raw Zone*. It was a test, limited to the Washington, D.C., area. The shows were in English. The ads were in Spanish. The results were spectacular. Hits on the Spanish-language portion of the company's website increased 300 percent.

The Takeaway

What does all this mean to you?

Here it is: Everything you want to do on the general market side, write it down. That's exactly the way you need to do your Hispanic marketing plan.

Don't go with billboards, Google pop-ups, prime-time TV, drive time radio, magazines, and Sunday newspaper inserts in English, then expect a one-time TV spot in Spanish to give you the same results. Work up a comparable plan. You don't have to match it dollar for dollar. Make it proportional, based on the demographics in the area you're trying to reach, and on your goals.

Speak to us in Spanish if you really want us to listen. Spanish speaks to us on an emotional level in a way English never can. We hear English, we *feel* Spanish. English reaches us, but Spanish moves us.

And don't keep waiting for the use of Spanish to fade away. Lots of people have been waiting a long time for that. It's not.

It's growing, in every age bracket. And that means it's going to keep growing for a long time.

Want evidence? How about all the above, and just for fun, how about Univision's viewership is up 146 percent among 18- to 34-year-olds in just the last five years. And nearly a third of all the country's Hispanics are younger than that.

The bottom line: Wherever you advertise in English, you should advertise in Spanish. Nine out of ten Hispanics watch at least some Spanish-language TV, listen to Spanish radio, or read a Spanish-language newspaper or magazine regularly.

We watch television four more hours per week per household than the general market (57.15 hours compared to 53.15), and listen to radio longer (22 hours and 15 minutes per week on average, compared to the U.S. average household of 19 hours). And even the Internet is becoming a viable medium.

If you really want us to notice, offer it in Spanish, that's the key. We like to be courted in the language we make love in: in Español, of course.

Do that, and you can tap into the fastest growing consumer market segment in the country, with nearly $1 trillion worth of buying power. But that's the next chapter . . .

Chapter 7

WE HAVE REAL BUYING POWER

Here's the bottom line: Hispanics have money. Lots of it. But we spend it differently than other folks in the U.S. do.

Economics 101

It comes down to this: As the Hispanic population in the United States has soared, so has our buying power. And it's growing nearly twice as fast as everybody else's. By 2010, the buying power of Latinos in the U.S. is expected to hit $1 trillion. That's up from close to $700 billion today.

Take that much in $1,000 bills, put them end to end, and it would go around the Earth two and a half times.

That's a lot of money. Put it all together and we would rank fourth among the states, behind California, Texas, and

THE NATION'S FASTEST GROWING HISPANIC CONSUMER MARKETS 1990–2004	
(percentage change in buying power)	
North Carolina	949.1
Arkansas	924.6
Georgia	709.5
Tennessee	664.3
Nevada	558.5
Minnesota	540.6
Alabama	515.0
Nebraska	472.6
South Carolina	455.7
Kentucky	452.9

Source: Selig Center for Economic Growth, Terry College of Business, The University of Georgia, May 2004.

New York. But in front of everybody else—ahead of Florida, Illinois, Pennsylvania, and all the rest. And ahead of every country in Latin America.

Money Matters

That kind of buying power makes a difference. Economists have noticed. You should, too.

In its report on America's minority buying power in 2004, the Selig Center for Economic Growth put it this way: "The immense buying power of the nation's Hispanic consumers is reshaping the retail and commercial landscape of the United States . . ." At today's clip, Hispanics will have more buying power than any other minority group in the country by 2008. Latinos already have more spending power than Mexico or Brazil. Or Australia.

And it's not just how much we have to spend that's growing. Our share of the pie is booming, too.

"The Hispanic market is the growth market of the future," Ricardo Lopez, president of East Brunswick, N.J.-based Hispanic Research, said. "Without the Hispanic market, there will

TOP 10 HISPANIC CONSUMER MARKETS IN 2004	
(in billions of dollars)	
California	198.5
Texas	119.3
Florida	63.7
New York	56.6
Illinois	31.3
New Jersey	26.1
Arizona	20.9
Colorado	15.0
New Mexico	13.7
Georgia	10.9

Source: Selig Center for Economic Growth, Terry College of Business, The University of Georgia, May 2004.

not be significant growth in the U.S. market in the next fifty years. In order to do business in the U.S., we have to pay attention to the Hispanic market."

What he's talking about is this: The buying power of non-Hispanics continues to decline as a percentage of overall consumer spending, while the Latino share keeps going up. In 1990, Hispanic spending accounted for 5.2 percent of the U.S. total, according to the Selig Center report. By 2004, the Latino share had gone up 54 percent, to 8 percent of the total. By 2009, the center predicts it will hit 9 percent, while the general market's share slides to 91 percent.

By then, our buying power will have reached more than $68,200 per family, up from $43,690 today.

And it's not just because there are more of us. We're getting wealthier. The number of Hispanic households making more than $100,000 a year is growing more than twice as fast as the general population, according to Enrique J. Moras, vice president of acquisition banking for Wachovia Corp.

Hot Spots

That economic clout is turning up with varying degrees of intensity across the country. In Georgia alone, Hispanic buying power increased eightfold in just a dozen years, from $1.4 billion in 1990 to $11.25 billion in 2002.

In North Carolina, the increase is even more staggering: It

went from $8.3 million in 1990 (that's million, with an M), to $2.3 billion (with a B) in 1999. In the Raleigh MSA alone, Latino buying power hit $472 million in 2001.

In Pennsylvania, estimates put Hispanic buying power at $372 million in 2004. It's expected to grow almost 25 percent, to $460 million, by 2009.

That's a lot. But it's slow compared to what's been happening in a lot of other states.

According to the Selig Center report, the top five growth states from 1990 to 2004 were North Carolina (a phenomenal 949 percent), Arkansas, Georgia, Tennessee, and Nevada. Considering that Georgia, Nevada, and North Carolina also rank, respectively, tenth, eleventh, and twelfth in market size, the report calls them "three of the most attractive Hispanic markets in the nation."

If You Build It

Some major corporations have already begun shifting their lines and their strategies to deliver products and services Hispanics want. And they're getting results.

After it started losing business to local Hispanic merchants in a Houston neighborhood that became 85 percent Latino, Kroger Co., the nation's number one grocery chain, converted its 59,000-sq.-ft. store there into an all-Hispanic *supermercado*.

It worked. Today, customers find Spanish-language signs

to welcome them, and catfish and banana leaves lining the aisles. Keying off that success, Kroger has expanded its private-label Buena Comida line from rice and beans to 105 different items, and sells them at its stores across the country.

Albertsons made a similar switch in Los Angeles. They used brighter color schemes, added new product varieties, and devoted 30 percent more space for fresh produce and fruit. They also added bilingual staff, bilingual signage, and in-store music featuring songs by Hispanic artists.

The result, in the words of Albertsons' chairman, CEO, and president Larry Johnston: "Sales are up by strong double digits, with some product categories up more than 100 percent, and we plan to expand the concept to other Hispanic neighborhoods across the country." Publix took its turn in 2005. It opened two "Publix Sabor" stores in Florida, with bilingual signage and staff, an expanded produce section stocked with tropical fruits and roots, and a deli offering seafood, rice, chicken fricassee, ox tail, and roast pork. To counter the tendency of Latinos to go to specialty butcher shops to get the thinner cuts of meat we like, Publix revamped its meat department to include custom cuts.

The redesign went beyond food. Publix included other services and products it knows Hispanics want: money transfers, bill payment services, calling cards specific to countries around the world, fragrances, designer jewelry, and handbags.

If You Don't Build It, We Will

Grupo Gigante, one of Wal-Mart de Mexico's chief competitors, saw the opportunity to follow some of its former customers across the border. Taking advantage of its name recognition at home, and the brand loyalty of Latinos, it opened three stores in Los Angeles in 2003.

That was just for starters. The company reportedly plans to have seventy-one stores in California, Texas, New Mexico, and Arizona by mid-decade.

Similarly, Mexican household-cleaner manufacturer Industrias Alen is parlaying the power of its brands with Hispanics here. Run by two brothers, Alfonso and Enrique Garcia (the Al and En in Alen), the company is basically the Procter & Gamble of Mexico. It produces some of that country's best-known cleaning brands, including the leading bleach, Cloralex, and a Pine-Sol-style cleaner called Pinol that has a jingle as well known to Mexicans as the Oscar Mayer tune is to most American adults.

U.S. distribution has gone well enough that the company now manufactures its products at two stateside plants, in New Jersey and Texas.

We're Number 1

Wal-Mart noticed. The nation's largest retailer specifically caters to Latinos, and it pays off.

Wal-Mart prints its monthly ad circulars in English and Spanish. It joined forces with Sprint to offer prepaid wireless service for Hispanics. And, like Publix, it offers money wire transfers.

Late in 2004, it added a line of Mexican folk art–inspired bathroom and tabletop accessories from cookbook author Zarela Martinez. At Wal-Marts in heavily Cuban South Florida, Cafe Bustelo and Pilon coffee brands outsell Folgers, the chain's top seller.

Fortune magazine asked America's top retailers to name their highest grossing store per square foot. Wal-Mart named the one in Laredo, Tex., serving customers on both sides of the border. America's number one retailer is also in first place in Mexico.

How important are Hispanics in the United States to Wal-Mart's plans? It's probably more than simple coincidence that the company named Eduardo Castro-Wright as its executive vice president and chief operating officer in January 2005. For the four years before that, he headed Wal-Mart's Mexico operations.

Changing Fashions

The world's largest retailer isn't the only one adjusting its inventories—and its thinking—to attract Latinos.

Sears saw the light early. It zeroed in on hot spots on the neighborhood level. An analysis turned up about 170 stores in predominantly Latino zip codes. They pumped up their Spanish-language advertising to see what would happen and got such a phenomenal return-on-investment that they're now one of the biggest players in the arena.

Sears was among the first to market credit cards specifically to Latinos. It even launched the Lucy Pereda Collection, a dressy women's apparel line named after the Cuban-born TV personality and fashion expert.

Its sister-company, Kmart, debuted its line of sportswear and accessories by Mexican singing superstar Thalia.

Now, JCPenney sponsors Latina model searches and added clothing lines with Hispanics in mind.

It's a good investment. Latinas spend close to 20 percent more on apparel than non-Hispanics.

It's also an opportunity. Latinas come in all sizes, but their body shapes tend to be short and curvy. Producing fashions designed with that in mind is a category sure to grow.

Faithfully Yours

Hook us and we're yours. Hispanics are fiercely brand loyal.

In a Yankelovich survey, 61 percent said "it's very difficult to get me to change brands once I find one I like." Almost as many, 58 percent, said "it's risky to buy a brand you are not familiar with."

That can work to your advantage. A survey by Research Data Design found that 85 percent of Hispanics prefer to buy a more expensive but trusted brand rather than a less expensive one they don't know.

Grupo Gigante knows it. Industrias Alen knows it. So does Procter & Gamble.

P&G has spent more time and money than any other advertiser reaching out to Latinos, building the bond. The result: Six of the twelve brands that P&G's ethnic-marketing division manages are ranked number one among Hispanics in their categories, five others are ranked second.

PepsiCo International is banking that similar product loyalty and brand recognition will work for it. It's bringing fifteen confectionary items from its Sonrics product line in Mexico into the U.S. Among them, chili-flavored lollipops with a mango-gum center.

Two of Colgate-Palmolive's best sellers with U.S. Hispanics are products it makes in Latin America, Suavitel and Fabuloso.

The company's calculations give Suavitel a 37 percent share of the U.S. Hispanic fabric-softener market and put Fabuloso at market leader for liquid cleaners, according to AdAge.com. It's not just big companies that are noticing. Andy Scheid, owner of the Andrew T. Scheid Funeral Home in Millersville, Pa., knows it firsthand.

A Latino family came to him in the mid–1990s. Pleased by his service, they recommended him. Word spread. Nowadays, Hispanics in the area call him "Mr. Andy." He's buried two or three generations of some of their families.

"If they consider you a friend, you're a friend for life," he told the *Lancaster Sunday News*. Statistics back him up. The Yankelovich Hispanic Monitor found that "brands tend to play a bigger role for Hispanics" than they do for other groups. Just look at a couple of the findings.

- 65 percent of Hispanics, compared to 41 percent of white non-Hispanics and 60% of African-Americans, feel that brands keep them in-the-know and informed about what's going on in the marketplace.
- Hispanics (48 percent) are more likely than white non-Hispanics (20 percent) and African-Americans (40 percent) to feel that brands let other people know where they are on the social ladder.

Only Where It Counts

P&G may be a big spender when it comes to Latino-targeted marketing, but it isn't wasting resources. The company focused on a dozen products, including Crest, Gain and Tide laundry detergents, Pantene shampoo, and Pampers.

We also spend a lot—and a lot more than non-Hispanics—on cleansers. The Hispanic detergent market equals $544 million led by two P&G products, Tide and Gain.

We also buy more consumer electronics—everything from digital camcorders to video games—than most others. And how about our over-indexing on toothpaste by 120 percent and disposable diapers by 180 percent. We obviously like to have our teeth clean when we are making babies.

That's all worth keeping in mind when you're planning your product offerings and your marketing mix.

Spending Patterns

Hispanics over-index in their spending on a variety of things, and knowing that can help you. Latinos spend significantly more on gas, motor oil, men's and children's clothing, footwear, housewares, sports, and toys.

In one of the largest annual surveys of Hispanics, *People*

en Español's Hispanic Opinion Tracker (HOT) survey, 6,000 Hispanics said they spent on average of $1,992 on clothing and accessories in the last twelve months, compared to $1,153 for general market consumers.

That won't show up in credit card data, though. Only 15 percent of the respondents said they used credit cards, compared to 40 percent of non-Hispanics.

We're more likely to have satellite radio and dish TV than non-Hispanics. We also tend to run up heftier monthly cell phone bills than most, by far. And we spend $30 more per week on groceries, on average, than non-Latinos—$117 per week compared to $87.

That ties in with our culture and family values. Gatherings and festivities revolve around food. And we tend to think of cooking as an expression of love and a way to pass on traditions.

Eighty percent of the respondents in the International Dairy-Deli-Bakery Association's 2000 report *The Sandwich Study: Consumer Attitudes, Buying Behavior, and Purchase Drivers* said they serve traditional meals on holidays such as Christmas Eve and Cinco de Mayo. Almost two-thirds, 62 percent, said they would like their supermarkets to offer traditional foods for those occasions. Exactly the same number said they would like their supermarkets to offer catering services for *quinces* celebrations, our version of a debutante ball.

Cutting Edge

Hispanics eat beef twice as often as non-Hispanics, in general. We like leaner cuts, cut thinner. We don't like it frozen.

It's the same story with pork. Latinos over-index on pork consumption by 152 percent.

Our tastes have an impact. One of our eating habits is rekindling a sub-category in the meat industry. Goat is one of the fastest growing agricultural products in the United States. It used to be raised mostly for export. Now none leaves.

"It has been a long time since we have seen an opportunity in the livestock sector where the demand for the commodity far outweighs the supply," Ohio State University extension agriculture specialist Dave Mangione wrote in the department's Spring 2003 newsletter. Publix was right on target when it went with the custom-cut meat sections in its Latin-oriented stores. Hispanics tend to go to specialty butchers. We want our meat fresh, cut for *churrasco* or *palomilla*. If Publix offers the same thing, it saves a trip. Eventually, we might come to think of Publix as the place where we go when we're looking for meat, instead of as the place we go for groceries and can also find meat.

The search for fresh meat (we're the same about produce) helps explain why Hispanics go to the store so much. The Food Marketing Institute found that Latinos make an average of 4.7 trips per week to the grocery store—a whopping 18.3 trips per month. Compare that to 2.2 trips per week and 8.8 per month for the general population.

Dollars and Sense

Food Maxx is putting that knowledge to use. They stocked one Sacramento store with heavily Hispanic items: tamales and jalapeños; *masa* mix; Corona beer; *arco iris* and *surtido rico* cookies; Jarritos soft drinks; cans of *menudo* (tripe and hominy) and *pozole* (pork and hominy); 25-pound bags of beans and rice; Oaxaca-brand cheeses; Mexican papayas and mangoes; tomatillos, pasilla chilies, *chayote* (pear squash), and *pico Diana* (sugar mixed with chili powder).

Now, in an area that's about 18 percent Latino, about one-third of its customers are Hispanic. "We are trying to get them in here, and once they get in here, we keep them," says store director Bart Brackin.

Remember him from the chapter on family values? His comments there are worth repeating: "They don't just shop for TV dinners. It's a family thing, they bring the whole family, Mom and the kids and Dad and Grandma, and they fill up the shopping cart."

He's right. The FMI survey found exactly that: More than half shop with another adult from the household and 15 percent shop with children.

Banking on It

It's not just grocers finding a profitable new niche catering to Latinos.

Upwards of seventy-five California banks now allow customers opening accounts to use Mexican *matricula consular* cards as proof of identity. The payoff: In the first six months after it began accepting them, Wells Fargo reported nearly 80,000 new accounts using the cards as I.D.

"We are trying to bring financial services to the Hispanic community," Wells Fargo spokeswoman Miriam Galicia Duarte told the *Sacramento Bee*. "We want them to open bank accounts, to succeed financially . . . this is just good business practice."

In Gainesville, Ga., the Gainesville Bank and Trust specifically targeted Latinos with a bilingual branch called "Banco Familiar." A Hispanic-owned and -run competitor, the United Americas Bank, opened in Atlanta in 1999. Foreshadowing California's *matricula* model, it dropped requirements for a Social Security number from customers opening non-interest-bearing checking accounts.

In every case, the core business remained the same, but modifications made it more attractive to Latinos.

Josh Diaz, head of the Banco Familiar branch, told *Georgia Trend* magazine that standards for calculating credit-worthiness had to be reexamined to accommodate new immigrants who might have steady jobs but little or no credit history.

"If you try to do loans using a statistical model based on credit score, you won't make loans in the Hispanic community," Diaz said. "You have to modify the business model so that it's relevant." It applies in banking, and beyond.

For the most part, the Latino market is made up of young families. They're in the acquiring mode. And, for the most part, those young Hispanics don't have established credit here. You need to be sensitive to that and help them establish credit. Whether you're in the appliance business or in the used car business, it's a market that will be very loyal. But they're going to need a little extra help because they don't have established credit.

Financial Services Get in the Game

While the banking community has understood the importance of reaching out to Hispanics, the Financial Services sector has been slow to move. That is changing as well. Led by a true champion of the Latino consumer, the head of diversity markets for ING is determined to change the way Hispanics think about life insurance and retirement. Ricardo Valencia will tell you that he knows that 40 million Hispanics are not going to be his customers. "But there are pockets of wealth within the marketplace, and those are our ideal target." He is determined to position ING in the right light to tap that wealth. He even goes on to state what few, if any, financial service marketers get.

"The end goal is that ING does not need a diversity practice. Once the financial services industry understands the power, magnitude, and potential of the U.S. Hispanic market, the industry will treat it as it treats the general market."

Young Blood

The youth of the Hispanic population has important implications. A full 34 percent are 18 or younger. More than half, 54 percent, are under 35.

That provides benefits and opportunities. Hispanic teens control $19 billion in spending power. This sector is expected to grow by 62 percent by 2020, compared to 10 percent growth for teens overall.

Latinos already over-index on video game purchases. Imagine the potential of this coming teen wave.

Also, 29 percent of Hispanic women are 18 to 34 years old—prime childbearing years. The Baby Boom is still shaping the American economy, as we noted before, but keep your eye on the Bebé Boom. Latinas tend to have children younger and to have more of them. That makes us big buyers of formula, baby food, and disposable diapers.

We're also big buyers of toys. In its Hispanic Study, Simmons Research found that Hispanics are 33 percent more likely to buy toys than non-Hispanics. More than two-thirds of Latino adults said they bought games and toys in the previous year, while just over half of non-Hispanics said they did. Toys "R" Us reports increased customer traffic in Latino areas. Hasbro, LeapFrog, and Milton Bradley have all caught on as well. They're aiming ads at Latina moms. LeapFrog has created Spanish and bilingual titles for its interactive LeapPad.

And more children are on the way. In 2006, births continued to contribute more than immigration to the growth of U.S. Hispanics.

GROWTH SECTORS

Some business areas that offer good growth potential thanks to Latino spending habits are:

- **Remittances.** Many immigrants send money back to families, generating business for financial services companies. U.S. Hispanics sent nearly $30 billion to relatives in Latin America in 2004, more than the combined total the region receives from international aid and foreign corporate investment. Mexico gets the most, $13.2 billion in 2003 alone.
- **Housing.** Latinos live for the American Dream, as we noted in "We Love the U.S.A." They want to own a home. One in five of the homes sold in California is bought by Hispanics. That's good news for homebuilders and mortgage lenders (and insurers, and furniture makers, and . . .). Analysts estimate that Latinos will need 4.6 million housing units

over the next twenty years. The number of traditional entry-level buyers (33-year-olds) will go up 12 percent among Hispanics by 2010, even as that number declines among other groups by 10 percent.

□ **Satellite and communications**. As we noted, Hispanics tend to have higher cell phone bills than non-Hispanics. Simmons found that, as a group, Latino adults are 36 percent more likely than the average American adult consumer to have a bill of $250 or more in the last month. They're 30 percent more likely to have a bill between $200 and $249. And our desire to stay connected to family in faraway places means we also tend to ring up good-sized long distance bills.

□ **B2B and office supplies**. The estimated number of Hispanic-owned businesses hit 2 million in 2004, with more opening every day. That's up 30 percent since 1998, with no signs of slowing. The total is expected to grow another 55 percent by 2010, to 3.2 million. With estimated total receipts already topping $300 billion, this growing sector is good news for Office Depot, OfficeMax, Staples, and other sellers of office products and services. These expanding businesses and startups need computers, software, and technicians; telephones, copiers, cars, and delivery trucks; stationery and custom printing; furniture; and everything else it takes to run a business.

□ **Prescription Drugs**. Hispanic spending on prescription drugs is growing at 13.2 percent annually, faster than the general market. In 2003, Latinos spent $14.1 billion in this category. We're younger now, and having babies, but we won't always be. Right now, children's medicines should do well. Later, we'll want cardiovascular medications and Viagra.

Putting It All Together

Cashing in on the buying power of the Latino market is a lot simpler than some would have you believe. The data is available. The market is there, and growing—not just in dollars, in share. The general market is shrinking. The Hispanic market is getting bigger. You can't afford to ignore it.

What can you learn from successful businesses that have recognized the value, and strength, of our buying power? Simple modifications to your product lines and services can yield a major return.

Do a survey. Find out from where your Latino customers trace their roots. Then bring in products they know from their home country: Malta Hatuey and Cuban crackers for Cubans, Polar beer for Venezuelans, *nopales* and *chayote* for Mexicans. Cheeses for all of them.

And it's not just about food. We need to cook it. Is it worth it to you to offer the utensils and cookware we use to make things our way? Things like rice cookers, tortilla pressers, *cazuelas, comals*, and *molcajetes*?

Apparel stores may see increased sales by adding more clothes for men and boys, and almost certainly by devoting more space for kids' clothes—we have more kids, we need more kids' clothes.

Bankers found success by dropping the requirement for Social Security numbers. Dropping the requirement that we show a major credit card as an I.D. might do the same for you. We don't tend to have them. Why ask?

What's your store credit policy? Traditional credit ratings may cut off a lot of worthy customers. New arrivals haven't had time to build them up, neither have younger ones. A lot of us fall into one or both of those categories, so sticking to traditional rules could slam the door in a lot of potential customers' faces.

That's worth keeping in mind if you're, say, a car dealer who relies on credit scores to make loans—and who can sell cars without loans?

The same is true if you're selling appliances, or furniture, or consumer electronics. If you want to sell higher ticket items to Hispanics, take a hard look at your credit rules.

Remember, the key is: We have real buying power. Think about what that means to you. Take a look at our spending patterns. It doesn't take an MBA to know that giving us what we like is a sure-fire way to increase sales.

<u>Conclusion</u>

There you have them, seven keys to unlock a $1 trillion treasure chest. You can use them all together, or use only the ones you think apply to you.

- ◻ We All Use the Same Dictionary
- ◻ We're Everywhere
- ◻ We Love the U.S.A.
- ◻ We Vote
- ◻ We Have Strong Family Values
- ◻ We Want to Be Courted in the Language We Make Love In
- ◻ We Have Real Buying Power

What's important is that you apply them. Keep them in mind as you watch the changing marketplace around you. Use them to think about your marketing plan, the product lines and services you offer, and the way you do business. The keys will help you assess the lay of the land and spot changes on the horizon. With them, you can avoid pitfalls and zero in on opportunities. Now and in the future.

Hopefully, **We All Use the Same Dictionary** cleared up one of the most harmful myths out there. While your competition is getting all hung up trying to figure out which Spanish accent to use where, you can get your advertising rolling with one Spanish—"Walter Cronkite Spanish." You'll reach the most Hispanics, in all age groups, in the widest area.

And, you'll save money. One national message can work for all.

If you're targeting a specific group or a regional area you can go with local parlance. But, otherwise, there are very few reasons to go down that road, even fewer good ones. Save money. Save headaches. Go with "Walter Cronkite Spanish."

You also know you should avoid using words that have made their way into English because you think you know what they mean. *Cojones* may work over a beer when English speakers are talking about The Rock's latest action flick. But use it in a Spanish-language ad and you risk offending more potential customers than you attract.

Those are all things that make the work of a translator so important. Don't trust software to do it. You want a good one, with lots of experience, translating into his native language. Preferably, get one who specializes in marketing or advertising. It takes a special mind-set to come up with the kind of word play that will touch the right emotional hot buttons and motivate people.

Now you also know the importance of using the same dictionary everywhere. Because that's the next key: **We're Everywhere.** We're not just clustered in ten major markets or four or five coastal states.

The "Hispanic Smile" has evolved into a "Wide-Open Grin." We're filling in the Heartland, flooding the South and West. In fact, if it weren't for Latinos, much of rural America would be losing population. Hispanics account for the demographic growth and the economic revitalization of small-town America.

That means that if you haven't noticed us yet, you may not be looking.

It's certainly not because we're just fading into the tapestry. We're mixing in, but not melting in. Hispanics tend to acculturate, but not assimilate. It's an important difference. Because of the ease of travel and communication connecting us with our countries of origin, because of the Internet and Spanish-language television, radio, newspapers, and magazines, and because of our strong attachment to tradition, we're holding on to our culture and our language much more strongly than immigrant waves of the past.

We're holding on longer, too, with as much as 35 percent of third-generation Latinos speaking some Spanish. That connection is even bringing a wave of retro-acculturation and an even larger bicultural and bilingual segment. In the 2006

Yankelovich MONITOR Multicultural Marketing Study, 71 percent of Hispanics said, "My roots and heritage are more important to me today than they were just five years ago." Well over half, 56 percent, said they "make a great effort to become more connected with my heritage."

The fact that we're everywhere means you can't forget the keys anywhere. The NFL caught on to what that means. It launched NFLatino.com in 2006 to help the league attract a whole new fan base—Hispanics who might love sports, but know *futbol*, not football. To reach them, "we knew we needed more customized offerings in Spanish that spoke to this fan base," said Peter O'Reilly, director of marketing for the NFL.

For starters, the site includes real-time NFL and team news, schedules, scores, and team standings. But it also features expert analysis by columnists Alejandro Morales and Adolfo Cortes and diaries written by Latino NFL players. For newcomers to the sport, it includes a section with explanations of NFL rules and terms.

It's not just that we're in more places, there are more of us every place. Part of the reason is immigration, but a growing part is because of procreation. There are more of us in our prime childbearing years, and we tend to have more children. Put the two together, and it adds up. We're a big and growing share of the United States, any way you count—sheer number, as a percentage of the total, as a voting bloc, and in the amount of money we spend.

And, because so many of us are young, the growth—and

the impact—only grows greater. Almost a third of the nation's 43 million Latinos are under 18. The number of Latino teens is expected to increase by 62 percent by 2010, compared to 10 percent for all others.

"We are at the tipping point of an emerging new lifestyle category that will greatly affect American and global culture. Young Latino Americans are in the process of innovating their own customized culture that encompasses music, language, fashion, food, entertainment, and beyond," added Sharon Lee, Co-President/Co-Founder of Look-Look. "It's an exciting time and this young community is absolutely aware that they are the next big thing." The influence was being felt just this past fall, when ABC debuted *Ugly Betty*, an anglicized version of a hit Colombian *telenovela*, *Yo soy Betty la fea*. Not only was the show an adaptation of a Spanish-language soap opera redone for an English-language audience, but the network—for the first time ever—hired a U.S. Hispanic ad agency to promote it. In Spanish! The print ads showed actress America Ferrara decked out as Ugly Betty, complete with thick glasses, braces, and bushy eyebrows. The tagline said simply, "*Tan fea que la hicimos en inglés.*" So ugly, we did it in English.

"The ads are a private wink to the Latin community," said Santiago Pozo, ad agency Arenas Entertainment's CEO. "It's a crossover dream."

Translation: It's our American Dream. We come here because **We Love the U.S.A.** That's a key. We believe the United States is truly the land of opportunity, where, if we work hard, we can succeed. We can own a home. We can send our children to college, because we believe in the power of education, and we want our children to get the best possible, so they can do even better than us. Because of the entrepreneurial spirit so many of us have, we're starting businesses at three times the national average.

You know what that means if you're a homebuilder or in any related field. You know what that means if you're in business-to-business, providing office supplies, telecommunications, or any of the other products and services businesses need. You know what that means if you're a private school offer tutoring, SAT preps, or college loan services. And, no matter what business you're in, remembering those aspirational themes in your advertising and marketing can't hurt. Show successful Latinos—in their homes and businesses, as doctors, lawyers, and other professionals—in your ads. Offer scholarships, sponsor a school, reward students for good grades. The fact that there are so many of us and so many of us are young is bringing the greatest demographic shift this country has seen since the end of World War II and the start of the Baby Boom.

Politicians know that matters. They get what the key, **We Vote**, means. But the key doesn't matter only to politicians, it matters to you. Because what's true about us as voters is true about us as people: Relationships matter. We put a lot of value in the opinions of people we trust. We like it when you try to speak Spanish, no matter how bad it may be. We take it as a sign that you care enough about us to try. That means a lot.

Keep what the politicians have learned in mind. Use similar strategies when you're dealing with us, and watch your business grow. Business isn't only about business to us. Take time to foster the relationship when you're not making a sale, either on a personal level or by getting involved with the community. Sponsor events, Little League teams, grassroots festivals.

Relationships matter to us, especially family. You know the key: **We Have Strong Family Values.**

Our family comes first. We stick together. We consult one another when we're making decisions. We care intensely about our kids. And Mom is the center of our universe.

Don't forget what that means to you. If you're selling to us, you're never selling to only one individual. It doesn't matter if it's a car or a deodorant, our family counts. Mom matters most. She's the gatekeeper. Don't try to sell kid treats to her children. Show her how good they are for them.

If you're selling cars, Dad likes to think he's doing the picking. Let him keep thinking that. It can't hurt. But make sure your sales pitch shows the whole family enjoying the safe and comfortable ride. Consciously or not, Dad's decision is going to be affected by the family's input.

Just take your cue from Wal-Mart, one of the smartest marketers in the world. Their tagline in English is "Everyday Low Prices"; in Spanish it is *"Para Su Familia Siempre"*—For Your Family Always. The English tagline is built into their copy, but the importance of family is built into their tagline.

That's true no matter what you're selling. Influencers are

particularly powerful among Latinos. If Tía Fefa got a rash using a stick deodorant once, she's going to work overtime convincing people in her family to use roll-ons. If you want to sell Secret to her niece, you need to overcome Fefa's objections.

Influencers can also work to your advantage. Because we stick together, we rarely go shopping alone. Aim some of your in-store promotions at the influencer, not just the target, if you want to ring up more sales to Hispanics. Use bilingual signage. And, if you do it well, you can sell to the influencer, too, and make twice as many sales.

Tradition is one of our strongest values. We respect our elders and their ways. So we tend to keep our cultural celebrations going strong, no matter how many generations our family has been in the United States. Albertsons saw a way to tap into that. This past summer it announced a customized *Quinceañera* Program, with online and in-store components, to help Latino customers plan and celebrate our 15-year-old daughters' debutante balls.

Tradition (and Tía Fefa's experience) also plays out in our powerful brand loyalty. We may do things because that's the way they've always been done, including bringing home Palmolive dishwashing detergent because our mothers use it.

Family values and the importance we place on tradition and our heritage helps explain why we keep our language alive through so many generations. More than a third of third-generation Hispanics, the U.S.-born children of U.S.-born Latinos, speak some Spanish. But even the ones who don't speak any connect with it on an emotional level. That's why you can't ignore the key, **We Want to Be Courted in the Language We Make Love In**.

It's the reason MTV Tr3s is running bilingual programming, and why ABC is running Spanish-language ads for an English-language series. It's why Nickelodeon started accepting Spanish-language ads on its English-language network, and the reason Chuck E. Cheese's jumped at the chance.

When the California Wellness Foundation wanted to get its message about teen pregnancy out to U.S.-born Latino kids, it used print ads in English. But the attention getter, the part it knew would connect emotionally with Hispanic teens and remind them of the importance of not letting family down, was a single bold word at the top of each ad: *Futuro. Salud. Educación.* Future. Health. Education.

"We know that most of these teens, and the policymakers we're trying to target, speak English, but we wanted to do something to connect to their roots and grab their attention," said Dawn Wilcox, public education director for the campaign and vice president of Ogilvy Public Relations Worldwide.

Keep all of these keys in mind when you think about the last one: **We Have Real Buying Power**. Our spending power is booming, along with our numbers. But it's not just because there are more of us. We're making more. Our buying power is growing dramatically in terms of total dollars. But it's also becoming a bigger and more important part of the nation's to-tal. Our piece of the pie is getting bigger, while everyone else's is getting smaller.

I don't have to tell you what that means. The same way more babies started being born after the first G.I.'s came home from World War II, some folks see where this Hispanic thing is leading: Every day there are more of us, with more money. We're closing in, and fast, on $1 trillion in buying power.

If you want some of that money, applying the seven keys in this book helps you know which pieces of the puzzle to look for, and what's important. They give you a leg up on the competition that's ignoring the massive potential of Hispanic U.S.A., the ones who think it's just too complicated, and the ones wandering lost because they have no idea what matters to us, or how to talk to us.

Because you have the keys, you'll leave them scratching their heads trying to figure it out. All you have to do is use them.

Could Not Have Done This Without Them . . .

I want to first thank Carlos Harrison; his ability to capture and bring to life our thoughts, concepts, and ideas is a real gift. Rene Anselmo, who was the father of Spanish-language television and whom I was lucky enough to work with and get to know as a friend. My mentor and big brother Joaquin Blaya, the programming genius who made Spanish-language television programming relevant. The Zubi family, especially Michelle, for her unwavering support for this project. As far as I am concerned, she is one of the most dynamic advertising executives in the country, in English or Spanish. Lionel Sosa, the advertising guru who counsels presidential candidates on Latino values, whose enthusiasm for this project was instrumental. Lou Agnese, whose world is in higher education, thanks to his challenges, this is a much better book. Sergio Bendixen, a pollster extraordinaire, no one knows more about the Latino mind-set in America than he does; his insights are always on point. Walter Sabo, the man who taught me the one truth in talk radio: "No Opinions, No Ratings." I have followed his advice in this book. Ricardo Valencia, *mi hermano*, heads up diversity marketing for ING, and he believed in this body of work so much that he became the anchor account for my firm. Raymond Garcia with the Rayo imprint at HarperCollins, without his support, you would not be reading this.

Last but not least, I want to thank you for your purchase. Besides obtaining a better understanding of the growing Latino presence in America, your purchase is helping a fantastic cause. 100 percent of the royalties from this book are going to ProMujer, a micro-lending organization based in New York City that is empowering women in Latin America. I encourage you to check out their site at www.promujer.org to learn more about this magnificent organization.

Very Special Thanks

Very special thanks to my Mom and Dad, my brothers Andrew and Eddy, and my very special sister, Betty, for your unconditional love. To Sergio Pino, for showing me how to dream big and get it done. To Angel Veliz, for an incredible friendship and showing me the importance of determination. To George de Cardenas, for showing me the importance of laughter. To Phillip and Johnny, for showing me the importance of not taking life too seriously. To Adrienne, for showing me that being alone can be okay. To Mimi, for showing me that you can learn to wish upon a star. To Isabel, you taught me a life lesson that I needed to learn. OC Moran, for having taught me how to play in the big game. And last but not least, to God in the heavens, you have blessed me beyond my wildest expectations.

Bibliography

Abel, David and Lynda Gorov. "To Help Son at MIT, Calif. Couple Collects Redeemables." *Boston Globe*, March 3, 2001.

Acosta, Gary. "Hispanic Home Ownership Increase NAHREP." *National Association of Hispanic Real Estate Professionals*, Feb. 15, 2002.

Acosta, Maureen. "Contributions and Issues of Minnesota's Latino Community." *Chicanos Latinos Unidos en Servicio*, June 2004.

Advertising Age. "Hispanic Fact Pack. Annual Guide to Hispanic Marketing & Media, 2006 Edition." July 17, 2006.

Ahrens, Frank and Krissah Williams. "Spanish-Language Media Expand. Broadcasters, Newspapers Pursue Fast-Growing Market." *La Prensa*, Aug 15, 2003.

Alba, Richard. "Bilingualism Persists But English Still Dominates." *Migration Information Source*, Feb. 1, 2005.

Albey, Rhonda. "Focus in in on the Markets You've Been Missing to to Broaden Your Business's Horizons" *Business Start-Ups Magazine*, March 1997.

AllPolitics. "Texas Gov. George W. Bush Wins in in Landslide." *CNN.com*, Nov. 3, 1998.

Almendarez Coello, Renan. *El Cucuy: En la Cumbre de la Pobreza.* New York: Rayo. 2003.

AOL/Roper Hispanic Cyberstudy. 2005.

Apodaca Jones, Rose. "The Ethnic Equation; with with an Increasingly Diverse Culture, California Is Becoming a Testing Ground for How Business May Be Done in in the Future." *WWD*, Jan. 22, 2004, 14B.

Arbitron Inc. "Hispanic Radio Today; How America Listens to Radio." 2004.

Archibold, Randal C. "For Latinos in the Midwest, a Time to Be Heard." *New York Times*, April 25, 2006.

Arndorfer, Jim. "Anheuser-Busch Creates New Ethnic Marketing Posts. Hispanic and African-American VPs Named" AdAge.com, Aug. 8, 2005.

Arvizu, Ray. "Hispanic Chamber Convention High in in Patriotism." *The Phoenix Business Journal*, Oct. 19, 2001, v. 22, i. 3, 63.

Associated Press. "Food Companies Going after Hispanic Families." May 10, 2006.

Atkinson, Claire and Ira Teinowitz. "Nielsen Revises National TV Households Count. Asians up 3.2%; Hispanic, 2.9%; African-American, 0.8%." AdAge.com, Aug. 26, 2005.

Atkinson, Claire and Laurel Wentz. "ABC Hires First Hispanic Agency of Record. Arenas Entertainment Will Market 'Ugly Betty,' 'Desperate Housewives.'"" AdAge.com, Aug. 14, 2006.

Atkinson, Claire. "First-Half Ad Spending on Hispanic TV Up 15%. Nielsen Reports Overall Spending Up 5.7%." AdAge.com, August 31, 2005.

Atkinson, Claire. "Telemundo Teams with Yahoo to Create Hispanic Portal. Espanol.Yahoo.Com and Telemundo.Com Rolled into New Site." AdAge.com. May 10, 2006.

Atlanta, and bureau reports. "Hispanic Nation: Hispanics are an immigrant group like no other. Their huge numbers are challenging old assumptions about assimilation. Is America ready?" *Business Week*, March 15, 2004, i. 3874, 58.

Bachman, Katy. "Univision Radio Parts with Top Host El Cucuy." *MediaWeek*. March 17, 2004.

Bash, Dana and Ted Barrett. "Democrats launch 'Six for '06' agenda. Party unveils campaign themes, says elections will be about Bush." *CNN*, July 27, 2006.

Bauder, David. "Univision Soars During Summer Doldrums." *Associated Press*, Aug. 2, 2006.

BBC. "Latino Challenger Is New La Mayor. the City of Los Angeles Has Elected Its First Hispanic Mayor since the Pioneer Days of the 19th Century." *BBC*, May 18, 2005.

Bendixen & Associates. "Ethnic Media in America: The Giant Hidden in Plain Sight." *Bendixen & Associates for New California Media in partnership with Center for American Progress Leadership Conference on Civil Rights Education Board*, June 7, 2005.

Bendixen & Associates. "The Hispanic Vote in the 2004 Election." Jan. 25, 2005.

Berger, Joseph. "Wave of Foreign TV Becomes an 'Emotional Outlet' for Immigrants." *The New York Times*, Feb. 23, 2004, 1B.

Billips, Mike. "Accent Is on Service." *Georgia Trend*, April 2001, v. 16, i. 8, 155.

Blaney, Betsy. "Texas Family Loses Both Sons to to War." *Associated Press*, July 26, 2006.

Boden, Natalie. "Adding 'Gasolina' to your Marketing Strategy: Four Tips to Reaching U.S. Hispanic Youth. *Hispanic Marketing & Public Relations*, April 20, 2006.

Bond, Paul. "El Cucuy Ratings Debate Rages. Sbs, Univision Battle for Spanish Drive Time Shares." *The Hollywood Reporter.* Feb. 12, 2005.

Booth Thomas, Cathy. "Lionel Sosa; The G.O.P.'s Message Man." *Time*, Aug. 13, 2005.

Bopp, Suzanne B. "Hispanics at the Store. All Levels of the Food Industry Are Taking Notice of a Growing Population Segment." *Food Systems Insider*, Sept. 1, 2004.

Branch-Brioso, Karen. "Chain Migration Boosts Hispanic Populations in Unlikely Cities." *St. Louis Post-Dispatch.* May 11, 2004.

Broder, David S. "The GOP Lag Among Latinos." *The Washington Post*, July 23, 2006, 7B.

Burch, Audra D. S. "Hispanics Settling into South Change Its Culture, Politics, Economics." *The Miami Herald* March 24, 2004.

Burns, John. "Underserved Ethnic Group Has Huge Profit Potential." HousingZone, http://www.housingzone.com/index.asp?layout=articlePrint&articleID=CA462685, Aug. 2, 2002.

Bush, George W. "No Child Left Behind." Presented at Latino Business Association Luncheon, Los Angeles, Sept. 2, 1999.

Bush, George W. "Remarks by the President to the Hispanic Chamber of Commerce." *Newswire*, March 19, 2001.

Business Wire. "Presidential Candidates to Appear on Univision's *Sabado Gigante*." Oct. 26, 2004.

Business Wire. "Trix Circo Mundial Tours Hartford and New York City." June 2, 2000, 1330.

Business Wire. "Yankelovich Releases the 2000 Hispanic Monitor Results." Oct. 26, 2000.

Campo-Flores, Arian and Howard Fineman. "A Latin Power Surge: A new mayor in L.A. A decisive showing in '04. Latinos are making their mark on politics as never before. Get used to it." *Newsweek*, May 30, 2005.

Campo-Flores, Arian. "A Town's Two Faces: Struggling with the pain of change, Rogers, Arkansas—yes, Arkansas—is a testing ground for Hispanic growth in America." *Newsweek*, June 4, 2001, 34.

Chameleon. "For Companies in the Modern World—Adapt Your Business. Further Information on the Mitsubishi Pajero SUV." http://chameleon-translations.com/Index-Companies-pajero.shtml.

Chavarría, Jesús. "HB500 Growth at 10-Year High." *Hispanic Business.*

Chavarría, Jesús. "The Future Clicks for Hispanic Media." *Hispanic Business*, December 2005.

Chunovic, Louis. "Spanish-Language TV Hits Stride at Upfront Market." *TVWeek*, May 26, 2003.

CIA World Fact Book. "Countries Ranked by Population 2005." https://www.cia.gov/cia/publications/factbook/rankorder/2119rank.html.

CIA World Fact Book. "Rank Order GDP (purchasing power parity)."

Clemens, Luis. "Next Gen Hispanics Reshape the Market. Cable Nets Cater to Young Latinos With Telenovelas, Music, Wrestling." *Multichannel News*, Feb. 13, 2006.

Clutter, Ann W. and Ruben D. Nieto. "Understanding the Hispanic Culture." *Ohio State University Fact Sheet.* 2000.

Coates, Ta-Nehisi Paul. "Anthony Romero,. The Champion of Civil Rights." *Time*, Aug. 15, 2005.

Consoli, John. "Univision, Telemundo Target Anglo Biz." *Media-Week*. April 17, 2006.

Corr, Amy. "Out to Launch." Mediapost.com. Oct. 15, 2003.

Crowe, Deborah. "Tuning In." *Hispanic Business*. December 2004.

Crupi, Anthony. "Hispanic Upfront: Nets Target $1.8 Bil." *Media-Week*. May 15, 2006.

Cunningham, Brent. "The Latino Puzzle Challenges the Heartland; Editors Are Dealing with a Vast Demographic Shift. North Carolina Is a Case in Point." *Columbia Journalism Review*, March–April 2002, v. 40, i. 6, 34.

D'Ulisse-Cupo, Maria A. "Hispanic Immigrants: Trials and Tribulations." Yale-New Haven Teachers Institute. 2005.

Deggans, Eric. "MUN2 Reimagined: The Future of Hispanic TV?" Hispaniconline.com. May 2006.

Deitz, Corey. "Milwaukee Gets First Spanish Language FM Radio Station: 104.7-FM La GranD." *Your Guide to Radio*, from a Next-Media release, Sept. 15, 2005.

Del Conte, Natalie T. "Out of the Shadows." *Hispanic*. March 2006.

Duany, Jorge and Felix Matos-Rodriguez. "Puerto Ricans in Orlando and Central Florida." University of Puerto Rico, Rio Piedras. 2005.

Eaton, Tim. "Morals pulled Hispanics' votes. President won over more in 2004." *Corpus Christi Caller-Times*, Nov. 7, 2004. 1A.

EconSouth, First Quarter 2005 [NEED MORE INFO].

El Nasser, Haya. "New Urbanism' Embraces Latinos." *USA Today*, Feb. 15, 2005.

El Nasser, Haya. "Recent Immigrants More Educated Than Predecessors." *USA Today*, Dec. 6, 2005.

Elliott, Stuart. "Networks See Telenovelas as Maybe the Next Salsa." *New York Times.* January 5, 2006.

Elliott, Stuart. "Nielsen Will Address Potential Undercounting of Minority TV Viewers." *New York Times.* March 24, 2005.

Fatsis, Stefan. "Fans Say ESPN's World Cup Coverage Deserves Penalty." *Wall Street Journal,* July 5, 2006.

Federal Communications Commission. "Broadcast Station Totals as of December 31, 2004." February 10, 2005.

Federal Reserve Bank of Atlanta. "Riding the Rising Wave of Hispanic Buying Power."[DATE]

Fitzgerald, Kate. "U.S. Hispanic Radio Industry Gains Traction. Consolidations and Rising Ad Buys Buoy Latino Stations." AdAge.com. Feb. 2, 2005.

Fitzgerald, Mark. "Rompiendo Barreras." *American Demographics,* Nov. 1, 2003, v. 25, i.9.

Food Marketing Institute. "New FMI Report Provides Food Retailers a Blueprint on How to Serve Hispanic Shoppers." May 5, 2002.

FoxNews. "Bush Taps Kellogg Chief to Be Commerce Sec'y." Nov. 29, 2004.

Franke-Ruta, Garance. "Minority Report: The frustration of some black and Latino operatives raises the question: How much longer can Democrats count on historic loyalties?" *The American Prospect,* July 3, 2005.

Frazier, Mya. "A Closer Look at a Wal-Mart Survivor. How HEB Grocery Co. Beat the Odds in Hispanic Texas." AdAge.com. April 18, 2005.

Frey, William H. "Three Americas: The rising significance of regions.

(Longer View)." *Journal of the American Planning Association*, Autumn 2002, v. 68, i. 4, 349.

Fuentes, Annette. "Immigration Backlash Goes Local." *USA Today*, July 28, 2006.

Gallun, Alby. "Tribune to Offer *Hoy* Free in Chicago." AdAge.com. Dec. 8, 2004.

Gamboa, Suzanne. "Hispanic lawmaker blasts English proposal." *Associated Press*, July 26,2006.

Garcia, Edwin. "Spanish Language Newscast Most Watched in Bay Area." *San Jose Mercury News.* Sep. 27, 2002

Garcia, Guy. "Influencing America: Hispanics aren't just in the mainstream, they're shaping it." *Time*, Aug. 15, 2005.

Garcia, Guy. *The New Mainstream. How the Multicultural Consumer is Transforming American Business.* New York: Rayo, 2004.

Gardyn, Rebecca. "Habla English?" *American Demographics*, April 2001, 54.

Geoscape International. "American Marketscape DataStream. 2006 Series Executive Summary Report." 2005.

Green, Eric. "Report Finds New Demographic Pattern for U.S. Hispanics." U.S. Department of State International Information Program. July 31, 2002.

Gregory, Sean. "Diapers For Fatima. Everyone Wants to Own the Booming Hispanic Consumer Market. Procter & Gamble Can Offer Some Lessons." *Time*, Jan. 18, 2005.

Grover, Ronald and Aixa M. Pascual. "*Mano a Mano* in Hispanic TV. With NBC behind Telemundo, rival Univision flexes its muscle." *Business Week*, Sept. 9, 2002.

Guzman, Betsy. "The Hispanic Population; Census 2000 Brief." U.S. Census Bureau, May 2001.

Hall, Lee. "Market Has Yet to Meet Demand." *TVWeek*, Nov. 25, 2002.

Halliday, Jean. "Ford Unveils First Truck for U.S. Hispanic Market. Signs Branded Entertainment Deal with Mexican Singing Star." AdAge.com. April 26, 2005.

Herman, Eric. "*Tribune* to Stop Charging for Spanish-Language Paper." *Chicago Sun-Times*, Dec. 8, 2004.

Hickman, Holly. "Spanish Language Station Ratings Robust in North Carolina." *Associated Press*, Feb. 04, 2004.

Hines, Cragg. "Political Community Abuzz About Latino Electoral Heft." *The Houston Chronicle*, Nov. 14, 2004, O3.

Hispanic America USA. "Hispanics in Americas Defense. Hero Street U.S.A." http://www.neta.com/~1stbooks/hero.htm. 2006.

Hispanic Market Weekly. "Al Punto Wins Kia Hispanic Account." January 24, 2005. <http://www.hmwonline.com.>

Hispanic Market Weekly. "Credit Cards." January 31, 2005. <http://www.hmwonline.com.>

Hispanic Market Weekly. "Gasoline Companies." January 27, 2005. <http://www.hmwonline.com.>

Hispanic Market Weekly. "Getting Them Young." January 17, 2005. <http://www.hmwonline.com.>

Hispanic Market Weekly. "Household Supplies." January 20, 2005. <http://www.hmwonline.com.>

Hispanic Market Weekly. "Office Supplies." Feb. 3, 2005. <http://www.hmwonline.com.>

Hispanic Market Weekly. "Toy Manufacturers & Toy Stores." March 3, 2005. <http://www.hmwonline.com.>

Hispanic Market Weekly. "Tuned In." March 7, 2005. <http://www.hmwonline.com.>

Hispanic Market Weekly. "Upping the Ante." January 17, 2005. <http://www.hmwonline.com.>

Hispanic Television Update. "MTV en Español Revamps to Reach Young Audiences." Oct. 25, 2005.

Hoag, Christina. "Bilingual channel to replace MTV en Español. MTV plans to win over U.S. Hispanic youth with a bicultural channel called MTV Tr3s." *The Miami Herald.* April 4, 2006.

Hoag, Christina. "Discovery enhances Hispanic market; Discovery Networks gets aggressive in the U.S. Hispanic market with two new channels and a new Hispanic division in Miami." *The Miami Herald,* April 22, 2005,

Hoag, Christina. "Hispanic Television Networks Booming." *The Miami Herald,* Jan. 10, 2005.

Hudson, Eileen Davis. "Los Angeles: Nearly half of the city's population is Hispanic, and Hispanic media is right there to serve it." *Marketing y Medios.* October 1, 2004.

Humphreys, Jeffrey M. "The Multicultural Economy 2004. America's Minority Buying Power." Selig Center for Economic Growth, Terry College of Business, the University of Georgia, 2004.

Ives, Nat. "Hearst Sees Pretty Bit of Business in Quinceañera. Teen Titles to Feature 'Miss Quince' Aimed at Hispanic Girls. AdAge.com. May 12, 2006.

Jackson, Ben. "Aspiring Hispanic Start-Ups Boast an Edge." *American Banker,* May 11, 2004, v. 169, i. 90, 6.

James, Meg. "Grupo Televisa Sues Univision." *Los Angeles Times.* July 20, 2006.

Jarboe Russell, Jan. "Grand Opportunity Party," *Texas Monthly,* March 2005.

Jelinek, Pauline. "Hispanics one-seventh of U.S. population. Hispanics are the fastest-growing minority in America, largely because of immigration and a higher birth rate." *Associated Press*, June 9, 2005.

Johnson-Webb, Karen D. "Midwest Rural Communities in Transition: Hispanic Immigration." *Rural Development News*, v. 25, n. 1, 2001.

Jonsson, Patrick. "Underground Soccer League Alters a Town." *The Christian Science Monitor*, Nov. 26, 2003.

Jordan, Miriam. "Volkswagen Rethinks Its High Testosterone Ads." *The Wall Street Journal*, March 17, 2006.

Kandel, William and John Cromartie. "Hispanics Find a Home in Rural America." Amber Waves, U.S. Dept. of Agriculture Economic Research Service, February 2003.

Kaplan, Paul. "Hispanics Gain Foothold in Middle Class." *The Atlanta Journal-Constitution*, July 13, 2003.

Kasindorf, Martin. "Immigrant Groups' Aim: Turn Marchers to Voters." *USA Today*, July 14, 2006.

Kasindorf, Martin. "Parties Target Hispanics in 4 Battleground States." *USA Today*, July 19, 2004.

Kerris, Anastasia. "John Kerry Local Political Ad Spending on the Rise—George Bush Scaling Back. Spending in Total Outpaces 2000 Campaign, According to Nielsen Monitor-Plus." Nielsen News Release. June 17, 2004.

Kiefer, Francine. "Bush Plans 2004 Wedding with Hispanics." *The Christian Science Monitor*, May 14, 2001.

Kielar, Kerry. "Nielsen Media Research Local Market Universe Estimates for 2004–2005 Season." Nielsenmedia.com/Nielsen news

Release. August 25, 2004.

Kirp, David L. "The Old South's New Face: A Rapid Influx Of Spanish-Speaking Immigrants Has Transformed a Georgia Town." *The Nation*, June 26, 2000, v. 270, i. 25, 27.

Klaassen, Abbey. "Hispanic Reggaeton Is Radio Market Bright Spot. Radio Groups Flip Stations to Hot Latin Hip-Hop Format." AdAge.com. Jan. 31, 2006.

Klaassen, Abbey. "MTV'S New Hispanic Networks to Be Called TR3S. Former MTV Español Becomes Bilingual Network in Fourth Quarter. AdAge.com. April 4, 2006.

Klaassen, Abbey. "XM to Launch First Spanish Satellite Sports Channel. Sports-Heavy Programming Seen as Big Lure for Hispanic Market." AdAge.com. April 26, 2005.

Klein, Karen E. "Does Your Business Speak Spanish?" *Business Week*, June 19, 2003.

Kochcar, Rakesh. "The Wealth of Hispanic Households: 1996 to 2002." Pew Hispanic Center, October 2004.

Korzenny, Felipe. "Key to reaching Hispanics: Word-of-mouth, Door-to-door, and Network Marketing." *Minorities in Business,*. January/February 2003.

Kurtzman, Laura. "Schwarzenegger Star Falls with Hispanics." *Associated Press*, July 22, 2006.

Lafayette, Jon. "Univision: Come to Where the Ratings Are. Spanish-Language Network Heads to Upfront Touting Impressive Gains in 18—34 Demo." *TelevisionWeek*, April 25, 2005.

Lang, Thomas. "The Hispanic Press: Still Waiting for Bush and Kerry." *CJR Daily*, June 17, 2004.

Larmer, Brook. "Hispanics Are Hip, Hot and Making History." *Newsweek*, July 12, 1999, 48.

Leal, David L. and Matt A. Barreto, Jongho Lee, Rodolfo O. de la Garza. "The Latino Vote in the 2004 Election." The American Political Science Association. January 2005.

Learner, Neal. "Beyond Salsa: More Grocers Cater to Hispanics." *Christian Science Monitor*, July 28, 2004.

Legislative Analyst's Office. "Cal Facts 2004. California's Economy and Budget in Perspective." 2004.

Lehman, Andrea. "Hispanic Children Growing Percent of Younger Generation." HispanicBusiness.com. Dec. 21, 2005.

Lehman, Andrea. "Hispanics Fill Over 41 Percent of Jobs Created Since May 05." Hispanicbusiness.com. June 2, 2006.

Lichter, Daniel T. and Zhenchao Qian. "Marriage and Family in a Multiracial Society." [SOURCE?]

Lightsey, Ed. "Hispanic Tide Lifting Economy." *Georgia Trend*, June 2000, v. 15, i. 10, 22.

Liu, Betty. "The Americas: Rivals feel power of Hispanic voters: Betty Liu explains why Bush and Gore are wooing the Latino vote with great fervour." *The Financial Times*, Oct. 4, 2000, 12.

Mallard, John W. "We are at a crossroads: Serving the Hispanic community." Delivered to the Annual Board of Directors Assembly of the North Carolina Bankers Association, Greensboro, North Carolina, March 25, 2002; *Vital Speeches of the Day*, June 1, 2002, v. 68, i. 16, 501.

Mangione, Dave. "Meat Goats, A Field of Dreams for Agriculture." *Farm Management Update*, Spring 2003.

Marcano, Cara. "Buzz Marketing Tested as Effective Approach. In their quest to transcend the 30-second spot, more brands turn to word-of-mouth firms." *Marketing y Medios*, Sept. 1, 2005.

Marketing y Medios. "Viewers' Choice. Latinos cite plots as reason to watch novelas." May 2005.

Martinez, Miriam. "Lionel Sosa: marketing visionary who changed political history: head of Garcia KS." *Latino Leaders*, Abril–mayo 2004, v. 5, i. 2, 50.

Mehlman, Ken. "Report Shows Hispanics Are Opening Businesses Three Times Faster Than National Average." Statement By RNC Chairman Ken Mehlman on U.S. Census Hispanic-Owned Business Report, March 21, 2006.

Mehta, Stephanie M. "Univision is Ready for Its Closeup. Let the Bidding Begin for the Star of Spanish-Language Media." *Fortune*, Feb. 28, 2006.

Meximerica Media. "Meximerica Media Expands Spanish-Language Newspaper Chain to Houston. *Rumbo de Houston* is a new route to reach the fifth largest Hispanic market in the United States." August 24, 2004.

Miranda, Carolina A. "Ysrael Seinuk: The Master Builder." *Time*. Aug. 15, 2005.

Mohl, Raymond A. "The *nuevo* New South: Hispanic migration to Alabama." *Migration World Magazine*, March–April 2002, v. 30, i. 3, 14.

Moran, Michelle. "Catering to Hispanic Consumers." *The Gourmet Retailer*, Feb. 1, 2002.

Moscoso, Claudia. "Census finds Hispanic home ownership high in Volusia, Flagler." *Daytona Beach News-Journal*, May 24, 2002, pNA.

MTV. "MTV to Super-Serve U.S. Latino Market with MTV Tr3s." April 4, 2006.

Mun2. "mun2 Latino Youth-Only National Study." Mun2tv.com. March 6, 2006.

Murr, Andrew. "The Survivor's Story: Antonio Villaraigosa likes building bridges. First, he had to find his own way over." *Newsweek*, May 30, 2005.

Murray, Mark. "Can GOP count on Latino vote? Views differ on whether Republicans can continue Bush's success." NBC News, March 21, 2005.

NALEO. "2004 Election Profile. General Election: November 2, 2004." NALEO Educational Fund, October 2004.

National Council of La Raza. "Memorandum: How Did Latinos Really Vote in 204?" Nov. 16, 2004. (Revised Jan. 15, 2005.)

Novelli, William D. "How Aging Boomers Will Impact American Business." Presented at Meeting of The Wisemen, The Harvard Club, New York, NY. Feb. 21, 2002.

NPN Market Pulse. "With growth of Hispanic population, marketers see new opportunities." May 17, 2006.

O'Driscoll, Bill. "More Hispanics realize dream of home ownership. Rate on par with blacks: Latinos lag behind Asians, Indians, whites." *Reno Gazette-Journal*, May 8, 2002.

Ordonez, Jennifer. "Marketing 'Speak English. Live Latin.' Once, those vying for Latino bucks and ballots bombed with bad translations. Today, savvy appeals help close the deal." *Newsweek*, May 30, 2005.

Orozco, José. "Latin Spice. As America's taste grows for zesty Latin food, the companies dishing it up are striking it rich." *Hispanic Trends*, November 2005.

Oser, Kris. "How Nextel Quickly Expanded Its Hispanic Sales. Stacey Crespo Details Intense One-Year Campaign." AdAge.com. May 25, 2005.

Oser, Kris. "MSN Launches Spanish-Language Video Site. Move

Expands Portal's Already Vigorous Latino Section." AdAge.com. April 26, 2005.

Palmeri, Christopher. "Online Extra: Here Come The Latino Home Buyers." *Business Week* Online, March 15, 2004.

Parks, Ted. "Landmark study examines Hispanic religion & politics." *Religion News Service*, May 28, 2001.

Parrott, Jeff. "Home ownership lags Hispanic growth overall. Some impressed, others bothered, by 29% rate of households owned." *Lafayette Journal and Courier*, Dec. 18, 2002.

People en Español's Hispanic Opinion Tracker (Hot), 2005.

Petersen, D'Ann and Laila Assanie. "The Rapidly Growing and Increasingly Diverse Population of Texas." *Texas Business Review*, June 2005.

Pew Hispanic Center and the Henry J. Kaiser Family Foundation. "The 2004 National Survey of Latinos: Politics and Civic Participation."

Potowski, Kim. "Spanish language shift in Chicago." *Southwest Journal of Linguistics*. June 2004, v. 23, i. 1, 87.

PR Newswire. "Hidden Facts in New Census Hispanic Data." June 13, 2005.

PR Newswire. "The Washington Post Company to Acquire Spanish-Language Newspaper." May 17, 2004.

Pratt, Timothy. "National Hispanic Groups Taking Notice of Nevada." *Las Vegas Sun*, June 22, 2001.

Publix. "Publix Sabor." http://www.publix.com/sabor/. 2005.

Quaid, Libby. "Food Companies Going after Hispanic Families." *Associated Press*, May 10, 2006.

Radelat, Ana. "Up for Grabs: Latinos are this election year's swing voters." *Hispanic Magazine*, October 2004.

Ramírez Magaña, Abel. "A Bicultural Bias." *Hispanic Business*, December 2003.

Ramos, Jorge. *The Latino Wave. How Hispanics Will Elect the Next American President.* New York: Rayo, 2004.

Ramos, Jorge. *The Other Face of America. Chronicles of the Immigrants Shaping Our Future.* New York: Rayo, 2002.

Ratcliffe, R. G. "Parties Begin to Realize Importance of Hispanic Vote." *The Houston Chronicle*, Jan. 11, 1998.

Reuters. "U.S. Immigration Could Spell Big Business." Jan. 22, 2005.

Rhyne, Mike. "Hispanic Market Overview 2005." Powerpoint Presentation at Cattle Industry Annual Convention and Trade Show. 2005.

Rivera-Nogales, Elaine and Cathy Booth Thomas-McAllen. "A Whole New World: Along the U.S.–Mexican border, where hearts and minds and money and culture merge, the Century of the Americas is born." *Time*, June 11, 2001, v. 157, i. 23, 36.

Rodriguez, Gregory. "Whey We're the New Irish. Mexican-Americans, too, began apart—and are now a thread in the tapestry." *Newsweek*, May 30, 2005.

Romero, Simon. "A Texas Paper Bets on Español, Not Assimilation." *New York Times.* January 31, 2005, 1C.

Roosevelt, Margot. "Antonio Gonzalez: The Get-Out-the-Vote Guy." *Time*, Aug. 15, 2005.

Rosenberg, Simon and Maria Cardona, Joe Garcia, Belen Mendoza. "Learning from the 2004 Campaign in the Hispanic Community." Hispanic Project, National Democratic Network Political Action Committee. Dec. 13, 2004.

Roslow Research Group. "Spanish vs. English Advertising Effectiveness Among Hispanic Teens." 2000.

Roslow Research Group. "U.S. Hispanic Population Projections, by Age & Spanish Language: 2005, 2015, 2025." Prepared for *Hispanic USA*. June 2005.

Ross, John and Ruben Martinez. "After Prop 187, new bonds of solidarity: youth achieve new political awareness." *National Catholic Reporter*, Dec. 9, 1994, v. 31, n. 7, 6.

Sanders, Tony. "Hispanic TSL Dips to 22:15." RadioandRecords.com, June 27, 2006.

Schacter, Jason P. "Migration by Race and Hispanic Origin: 1995 to 2000." U.S. Census, October 2003.

Segal, Adam J. "Total 2004 Spanish-Language TV Ad Spending by Market and Campaign." Hispanic Voter Project at Johns Hopkins University. February 2006.

Segal, Adam. "Records Broken: Spanish-Language Television Advertising in the 2002 Election." Hispanic Voter Project, Johns Hopkins University. Nov. 21, 2002.

Sepulveda Jr., Juan A. *The Life and Times of Willie Velasquez. Su Voto Es Su Voz.* Houston: Arte Publico Press, 2003.

Sherman, Christopher. "Florida Hispanics' Labor Aids Families Back Home in Latin America." *The Orlando Sentinel*, May 18, 2004.

Shields, Mike. "Univision Google Make Search Pact." *Mediaweek*, July 28, 2005.

Shields, Mike. "Yahoo, NBCU Create Yahoo Telemundo." *Mediaweek*, May 10, 2006.

Shoer-Roth, Daniel. "Univision pioneer working on Mideast. Joaquín Blaya is polishing the U.S. reputation in the Middle East via TV and radio." *El Nuevo Herald*, July 10, 2006.

Shrestha, Laura B. "The Changing Demographic Profile of the United States." Congressional Research Service, Library of Congress. Updated May 5, 2006.

Simao, Paul. "Hispanics Flex New Muscle in US." Reuters News Service, via *The Financial Gazette*, June 27, 2002.

Simmons, an Experian Company. "Analysis of Hispanic Buying Patterns for José Cancela." 2005.

Smart, Gil. "Bilingualism and the bottom line. Led by car dealers, local businesses are learning that catering to Latino customers can boost sales." Sunday NewsLancasterOnline.com, March 5, 2005.

Sneddon Little, Jane and Robert K. Triest. "Seismic Shifts: The Economic Impact of Demographic Change. An Overview." Conference Series—Federal Reserve Bank of Boston. 2001.

Sorkin, Andrew Ross. "In Late Twist, Univision Accepts Bid." *New York Times*, June 27, 2006.

South Florida Sun-Sentinel/El Sentinel. "Sun-Sentinel to Publish Weekly Spanish Language Newspaper." Aug. 16, 2002.

South, Jeff and David Kennamer. "Adapting to rapid change: community papers respond to Latino immigration. (Varying the Voice)." *The Quill*, March 2003 v91 i2 p30.

South, Jeff and David Kennamer. "Adapting to Rapid Change: Community Papers Respond to Latino Immigration. *The Quill*, March 2003, v. 91, i. 2, 30.

Southern Methodist University Tower Center. "John G. Tower Biography." www.smu.edu/tower/biography.asp?.

Spanish Broadcasting System, Inc. "Corporate History." Spanishbroadcasting.com. 2001.

Steptoe, Sonja. "Pablo Alvarado: The New Cesar Chavez." *Time*, Aug. 15, 2005.

Streisand, Betsy. "Latino Power: Big media tune in to the nation's largest minority." *US News & World Report.* March 17, 2003.

Suro, Roberto and Audrey Singer. "Latino Growth in Metropolitan America: Changing Patterns, New Locations." The Brookings Institution Center on Urban & Metropolitan Policy and The Pew Hispanic Center, July 2002.

Suro, Roberto and Gabriel Escobar. "2006 National Survey of Latinos: The Immigration Debate." Pew Hispanic Center, July 13, 2006.

Suro, Roberto and Jeffrey S. Passel. "The Rise of the Second Generation: Changing Patterns in Hispanic Population Growth." Pew Hispanic Center and Urban Institute, October, 2003.

Suro, Roberto, et al. "Hispanics: A People in Motion." Pew Hispanic Center, 2005.

Sutel, Seth. "Newsweeklies Rarely Cover Hispanics." InsideVC.com, June 14, 2006.

Swarns, Rachel L. "Children of Hispanic Immigrants Continue to Favor English, Study of Census Finds." *New York Times,* Dec. 8, 2004.

Szalai, Georg and Paul Bond. "Cascade Joins Univision Parade." *The Hollywood Reporter,* May 15, 2006.

Taylor, Chris. "Sara Martinez: Tucker The College Recruiter." *Time,* Aug. 15, 2005.

The Brookings Institution. "U.S. Latino Population Growth Extends Far Beyond Established Hubs, Center Cities. Study Reveals New Geography of Latinos in America." July 31, 2002.

The Project for Excellence in Journalism. "The State of the News Media 2004; Ethnic/Alternative." Journalism.org, 2004.

Therrien, Melissa and Roberto R. Ramirez. "The Hispanic Population in the United States, March 2000." U.S. Census, issued March 2001.

Thomaselli, Rich and Laurel Wentz. "Reebok to Launch Daddy Yankee Shoe; Hispanic Reggaeton Music Star Expands Endorsement Push." AdAge.com, March 6, 2006.

Thomaselli, Rich. "Spanish Version of 'ESPN The Magazine' Planned. ESPN Partners With Editorial Televisa for Launch." AdAge.com, March 16, 2005.

Tucker, Ken. "CC Changes WEBG-FM from Oldies to Hispanic." *Billboard*, Feb. 2, 2005.

U.S. Census Bureau. "2005 American Community Survey." 2006.

U.S. Census Bureau. "Facts for Features, Hispanic Heritage Month, Sept. 15–Oct. 15, 2006." July 26, 2006.

U.S. Census Bureau. "Florida, California & Texas Dominate Future Population Growth." April 25, 2005.

U.S. Census Bureau. "Hispanic Americans by the Numbers." 2006.

U.S. Census Bureau. "Hispanic and Asian Americans Increasing Faster than Overall Population." June 14, 2004.

U.S. Census Bureau. "Hispanic Population Passes 40 Million, Census Bureau Reports." June 9, 2005.

U.S. Census Bureau. "Nation's Population One-Third Minority." May 10, 2006.

U.S. Census Bureau. "Selected Age Groups for the Population by Race and Hispanic Origin for the United States: July 1, 2005." 2006.

U.S. Census Bureau. "Statistical Abstract of the United States." http://www.census.gov/prod/www/statistical-abstract–04.html. Dec. 8, 2005.

U.S. Department of Agriculture. "Rural Hispanics at a Glance." *Eco-*

nomic Information Bulletin, December 2005.

U.S. Department of Defense Federal Voting Assistance Program. "Federal Elections and Officials." http://www.fvap.gov/comm/cw-yeo.html.

U.S. Department of Labor. "Consumer Expenditure Survey, 2004."

Ulibarri, Carlos. "Marketing to Affluent Hispanics Is More than Marketing Communications." http://www.cheskin.com/blog/blog/archives/000403.html, June 9, 2004.

Unilever. "Winning the Hispanic Shopping Trip. A Unilever Trip Management Report." 2006.

Univision Communications Inc. "Univision unveils consumer research on the who, why and how of Spanish language TV." March 3, 2004.

Univision. "First Time Ever Spanish TV Station Leads Tucson." March 28, 2005.

Univision. "Gotham TV Viewers Flock to Univision TV Stations in February Sweep." March 4, 2004.

Univision. "Univision Draws More Viewers—Hispanic or Non-Hispanic—Than 5 English Language Networks." Oct. 28, 2004.

Univision. "Univision Stations #1 All Day in Nation's Top 3 Television Markets Among All Adults 18–34 In Nielsen NSI March Sweep." May 13, 2002.

Ureel, Mike. "Padilla Retires After Long, Successful Career with Ford." *Ford Corporate News*. June 30, 2006.

Vargas, Arturo. "Latino Voters." *Vital Speeches of the Day*, Jan 1, 2000, v. 66, i. 6, 170.

Vargas, José Antonio. "Spanish Ads on English TV? An Experiment." *Washington Post*, May 31, 2005, 1C.

Vasquez, Beverly. "Hispanics Leading in Business Growth." *Denver Business Journal*, Sept 13, 1996, v. 48, n. 1, 1A.

Waldman, Alan and Bill Knight. "The Top 15 Hispanic Markets." *Multichannel News*, Oct. 30, 2000, v. 21, i. 44, 10A.

Waller, J. Michael. "Hispanic Voters." *Insight on the News*, Nov. 6, 2000, v. 16, i. 41, 10.

Washington Post/Univision/Tomás Rivera Policy Institute. "Election Survey of Latino Registerd Voters, July 2004."

Weldon Cooper Center for Public Service,University of Virginia. "Growth in the Latino/Hispanic Population—Analysis." http://www.coopercenter.org/demographics/ANALYSIS%20%26%20GRAPHICS/Hispanic%20Population/Analysis/index.php. 2005.

Wentz, Laurel. "Ford Backs AOL Latino City Guide Hub. Spanish-Language Guide to 16 Cities." AdAge.com, April 18, 2005.

Wentz, Laurel. "Hearst, Grupo Reforma Launch Spanish-Language Paper. Mexican Publisher Modeling Its U.S. Expansion on Univision Strategy." AdAge.com, June 5, 2006.

Wentz, Laurel. "Hershey's Product Name Sparks Hispanic Controversy. New Cajeta Candy Aimed at Mexicans Rather than All U.S. Latinos." AdAge.com, Feb. 22, 2005.

Wentz, Laurel. "Hispanic Ad Agencies Eye More Digital Accounts. Half of Hispanic Online Ad Work Still Controlled by General Agencies." AdAge.com, May 6, 2005.

Wentz, Laurel. "Hispanic Media to Grow 11% in 2005. Again Outpace Mainstream Media's 4% Annual Growth Rate." AdAge.com, Jan. 31, 2005.

Wentz, Laurel. "Investment Group Buys Univision for $13.7 Billion. Mexico's Grupo Televisa Fails to Acquire U.S. Spanish-language Network." AdAge.com, June 27, 2006.

Wentz, Laurel. "J&J Hits Road In Search Of Hispanic Connections.

Mobile Exhibit Starts 34-Week National Wal-Mart Parking Lot Tour." AdAge.com, March 21, 2005.

Wentz, Laurel. "Latino Magazines Are Proving Their Online Potential.' 'Latina' and 'People en Espanol' Sites Grow Rapidly." AdAge.com, Sept. 4, 2006.

Wentz, Laurel. "Mexican Marketers Push Further into U.S. Exploit Broad U.S. Hispanic Market for Familiar Household Products." AdAge.com, May 16, 2005.

Wentz, Laurel. "Rapid Change Sweeps Hispanic Advertising Industry. Shifting Demographics Alter Comfortable Assumptions and Business Environment." AdAge.com, May 3, 2005.

Wentz, Laurel. "Spanish-Language TV Spending Spiked in Late 2005. TNS: It Soared 20.3% in September; Stayed High Through 4th Quarter. AdAge.com, March 07, 2006.

Wentz, Laurel. "Televisa May Look for New U.S. Spanish-Language TV Ventures. Univision's Sale of U.S. Network to Investment Group Angers Mexican Media Company." AdAge.com, July 06, 2006.

Wentz, Laurel. "Tough Lessons in Ethnic Outreach: Pfizer, Other Drug Giants Still in Learning Phase of Connecting Multiculturally." *Advertising Age*, Nov 15, 2004, v. 75, i. 46, 36.

Wheat, Alynda. "Where are the best stores in the United States? FORTUNE 500 Retail Champs." *Fortune*, April 25, 2001.

Whitefield, Mimi. "Stouffer's courts Hispanics with frozen foods." *The Miami Herald*, July 15, 2002, 14G.

Whitney, Daisy. "AOL Expands IN2TV into Spanish." *TV Week*, July 19, 2006.

Wiegand, Steve. "Latino Population's Buying Clout Rises, But Income Lags in California." *The Sacramento Bee*, Sept. 16, 2003.

Williams, A.R. "Latinos Rise Nationwide. America's new major-ity minority." National Geographic Geographica, http://magma.nationalgeographic.com/ngm/0311/resources_geo.html, November 2003.

Wiltz, Teresa and Paul Farhi. "Alternative Rock Pioneer Targets La-tino Audience." *Washington Post.* January 13, 2005, 1A.

Woods, Bob. "Takin' It to the Streets." *PRIMEDIA Business Maga-zines & Media Inc.* May 1, 2000.

www.medalofhonor.com. "Congressional Medal of Honor—His-panic Military Heroes." 2006.

York, Anthony. "Can Bush carry California? He'll need the support of Latinos, but his campaign is giving mixed signals about how hard it plans to fight." Salon.com, March 13, 2000.

York, Anthony. "The GOP's Latino strategy." Salon.com, Jan. 14, 2000.

York, Anthony. "Viva Iowa." Salon.com, Oct. 25, 1999.

York, Anthony. "You Gotta Have Corazón." Salon.com, April 7, 2000.

Zimmerman, Ann. "Wal-Mart's Efforts to Attract More Hispanic Customers Appear to be Paying Off." *The Wall Street Journal,* June 6, 2005.

Zogby, Joe and Rebecca Wittman. "Hispanic Perspectives, Submit-ted to the National Council of La Raza." June 2004.

DATE			